SOUTHWESTERN INDIAN TRIBES

by *TOM BAHTI*

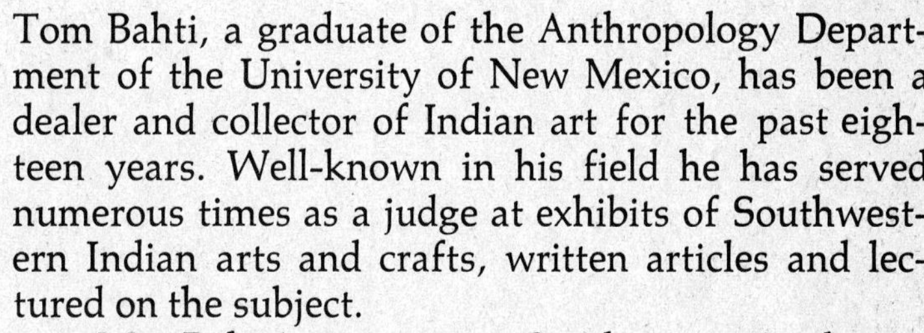

Tom Bahti, a graduate of the Anthropology Department of the University of New Mexico, has been a dealer and collector of Indian art for the past eighteen years. Well-known in his field he has served numerous times as a judge at exhibits of Southwestern Indian arts and crafts, written articles and lectured on the subject.

Mr. Bahti's interest in Southwestern tribes is not limited to their crafts, however, as he is also active in several organizations which seek to improve the general welfare of the Indians through self-help programs.

An Arizonian by choice, he resides in Tucson where he owns and operates an Indian arts and crafts shop. He is also the author of the book, *Southwestern Indian Arts and Crafts.*

Zuni Shalako kachina doll.

INDEX OF INDIAN TRIBES

Third printing, 1971

PUBLISHED BY KC PUBLICATIONS, BOX 14883, LAS VEGAS, NEVADA, • L. OF C. NUMBER 68-31188
SOFT COVER EDITION, TWO DOLLARS • BOOK DESIGN BY ROBERT JACOBSON

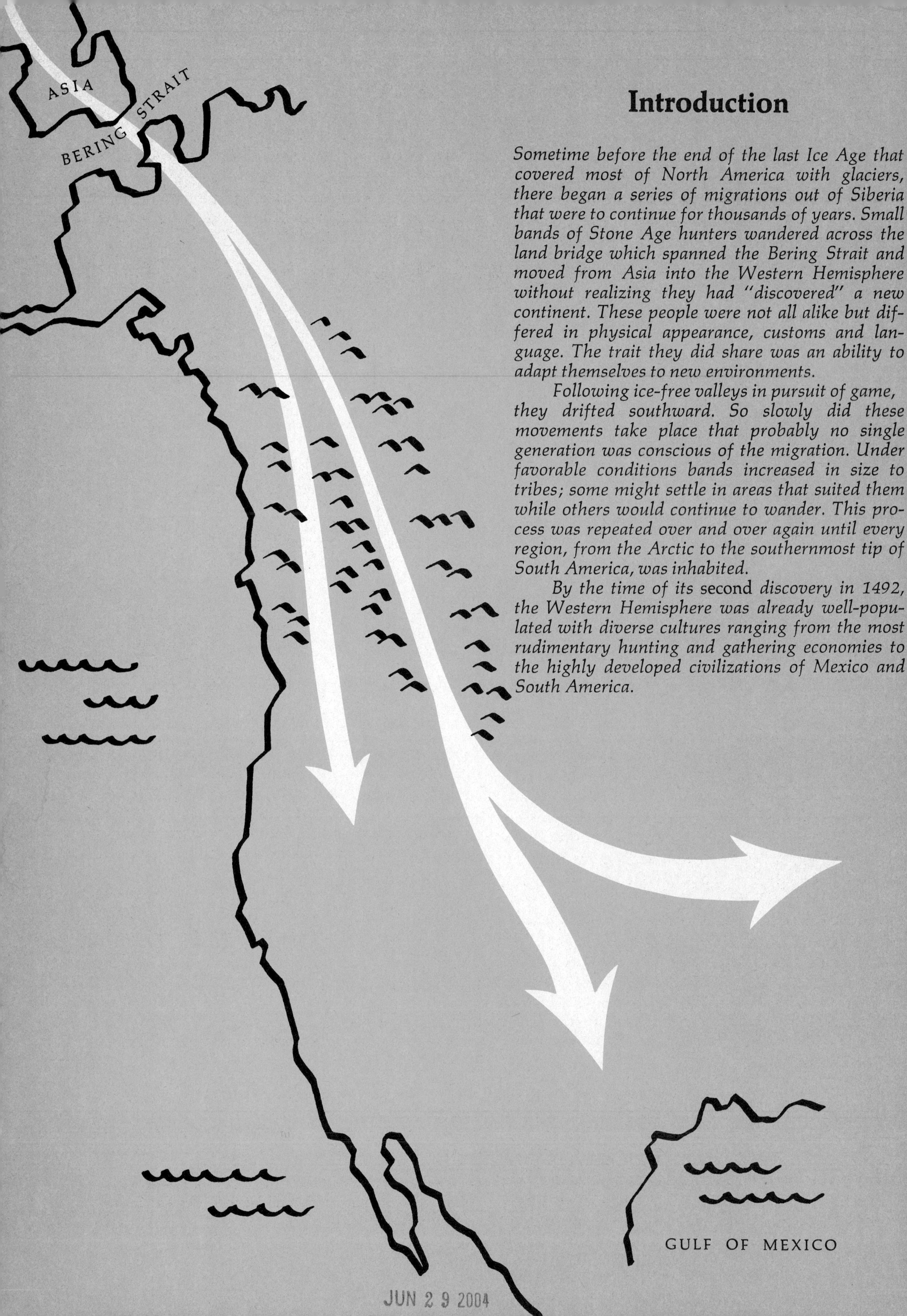

Introduction

Sometime before the end of the last Ice Age that covered most of North America with glaciers, there began a series of migrations out of Siberia that were to continue for thousands of years. Small bands of Stone Age hunters wandered across the land bridge which spanned the Bering Strait and moved from Asia into the Western Hemisphere without realizing they had "discovered" a new continent. These people were not all alike but differed in physical appearance, customs and language. The trait they did share was an ability to adapt themselves to new environments.

Following ice-free valleys in pursuit of game, they drifted southward. So slowly did these movements take place that probably no single generation was conscious of the migration. Under favorable conditions bands increased in size to tribes; some might settle in areas that suited them while others would continue to wander. This process was repeated over and over again until every region, from the Arctic to the southernmost tip of South America, was inhabited.

By the time of its second *discovery in 1492, the Western Hemisphere was already well-populated with diverse cultures ranging from the most rudimentary hunting and gathering economies to the highly developed civilizations of Mexico and South America.*

Early Man in the Southwest

The story of man in the Southwest begins about 25,000 years ago with the appearance of small bands of nomads who hunted with spears the mammoth, camel, bison, and ground sloth. Evidence of their passing is found only in the stone implements they made and left in their caves and campsites, often imbedded in the skeletal remains of the animals they killed.

With the retreat of the glaciers the climate slowly changed. The once lush land which supported the herds of animals these people hunted became progressively drier. Lakes and swamps disappeared and streams ran intermittently. Once plentiful game diminished, and man was forced to alter his way of life to meet these changes in his environment. He began to supplement his diet of meat by gathering seeds and edible plants. As plant foods became increasingly important in his diet, man developed the rudiments of agriculture.

Agriculture does not allow a nomadic existence, so man built semi-permanent dwellings near his fields. Villages soon followed and with them came all of the complexities of social and religious life that occur when men live together in communities.

Not all groups developed at the same pace but contact between them increased and new ideas were exchanged. Basketry and weaving were highly developed and widespread. Pottery, a craft usually associated with sedentary, agricultural people, was either invented independently or introduced from Mexico around the beginning of the Christian era; by 600 A.D. it was known throughout the Southwest.

Movements of people still occurred, however, as local populations were subjected to drouths, erosion of farmlands, internal conflicts, or merely the human urge to move to a new area.

Cultivation of the Sacred Triad — maize, squash, and beans — now provided a stable food supply and populations and villages increased in size and number. Social organization, ceremonialism, architecture, and crafts became more complex. Trade with the civilizations of Mexico grew and further enriched the life of these people. By 1000 A.D. these village dwellers, or pueblo Indians, had reached a "golden age".

Shortly after this the ancestors of the Athabascan-speaking Navajo and Apache entered the Pueblo domain. Their constant raiding forced the pueblo farmers to fortify their towns or to abandon them entirely. By 1250 A.D. many of the great pueblos were deserted and the people sought refuge in the Rio Grande valley and the vicinity of Acoma and Zuni.

A prolonged drouth in the late 1200's added to the pueblo people's problems and resulted in more forced migrations. When the Spaniards arrived on the scene most of the pueblo population was concentrated at Hopi, Zuni, Acoma, and in the Rio Grande valley.

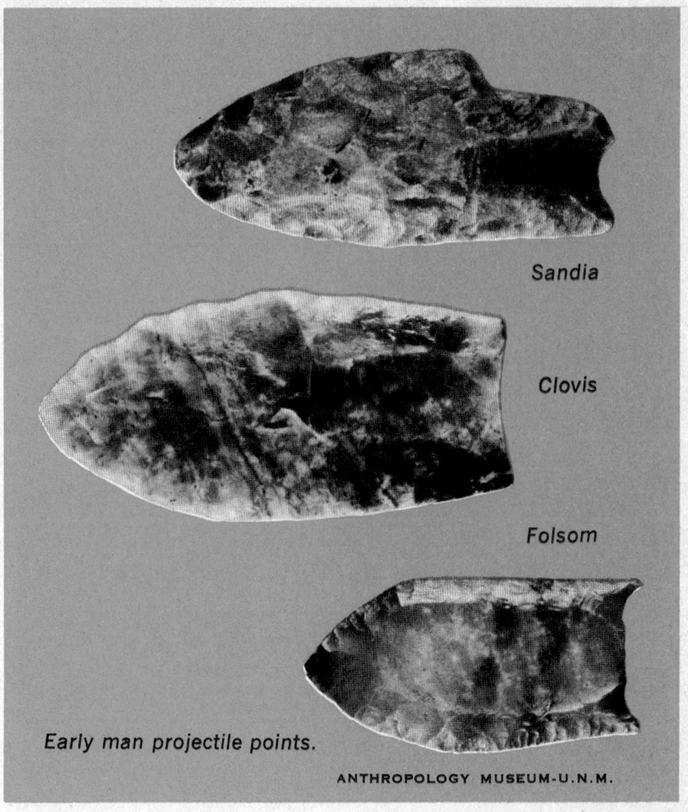

Early man projectile points.

ANTHROPOLOGY MUSEUM-U.N.M.

At about this same time (1200 A.D.) the Piman-speaking tribes, who are probably the descendants of the earlier Hohokam people, occupied southern Arizona, and Yuman-speaking groups moved eastward from California into Arizona and settled along the Colorado River.

By the late 1600's most of these tribes were occupying the same areas they do today with the Navajo and Apache people moving into the intervening areas.

SUGGESTED READING

Hibben, Frank C. *The Lost Americans.* Thomas Y. Crowell Co. N. Y. 1968.

McGowan, Kenneth and Joseph Hester Jr. *Early Man in the New World.* Doubleday & Co. Garden City, N. Y. 1962.

Wormington, H.M. *Ancient Man in North America.* Colorado Museum of Natural History, Popular Series No. 4. Denver, 1957.

Wormington, H.M. *Prehistoric Indians of the Southwest.* Colorado Museum of Natural History, Popular Series, No. 7 Denver, 1947.

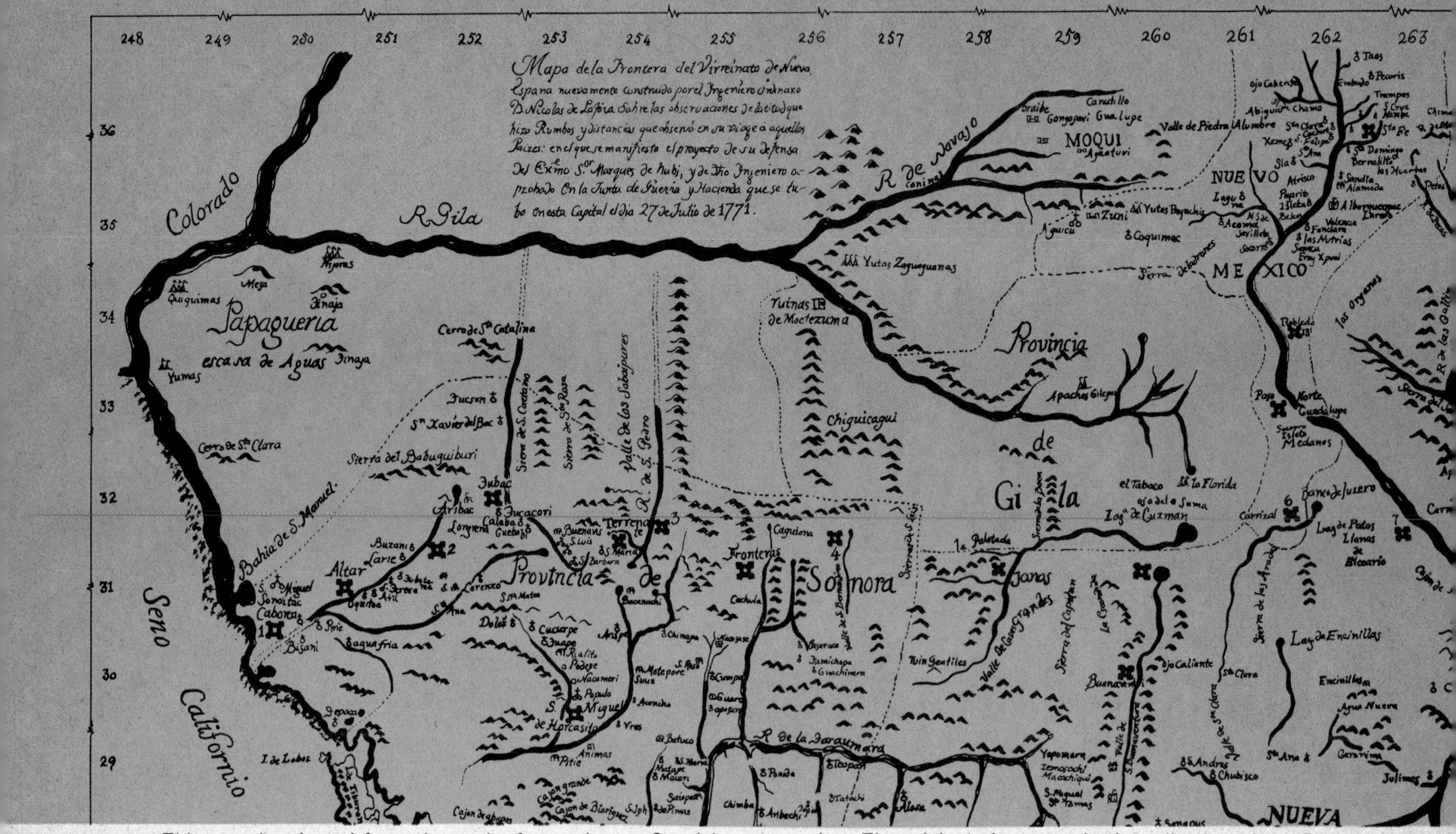

This map is adapted from the work of an unknown Spanish cartographer. The original chart, now in the collection of the British Museum, was probably part of the booty taken from a Spanish Ship by a British privateer.

European Contact

The search for Cibola, a mythical province containing seven cities of silver and gold, brought the Spanish conquistadores to the Southwest. A series of explorations, begun in 1539 by Fray Marcos de Niza, failed to locate anything more spectacular than villages of mud and stone inhabited by people rich in ceremonialism but poor in material possessions.

Formal colonization of New Mexico was begun in 1598 under the leadership of Don Juan de Onate. The pueblo Indians were required to swear obedience to the King of Spain and the Catholic church. The Indians were not ousted from their lands as the Spaniards preferred to have them remain to be exploited by civil and church authorities. Tribute was demanded in the form of forced labor, food, crops, buckskin, and textiles. In return each pueblo received a Spanish name, religious instruction, and promise of military protection from marauding tribes. Of far greater importance to the Indians was the acquisition of iron tools, fruit trees, new domestic plants, cattle, horses, and sheep.

The Spaniards also imposed the Law of the Indies which decreed that each village elect a governor, lieutenant governor, and other officials to handle secular affairs. The Indians obligingly added this new political system to their theocratic form

The governor of Taos holds one of the silver headed canes presented by President Lincoln to pueblo leaders in 1863. Many Rio Grande pueblos retain these canes as symbols of authority for the village governors.

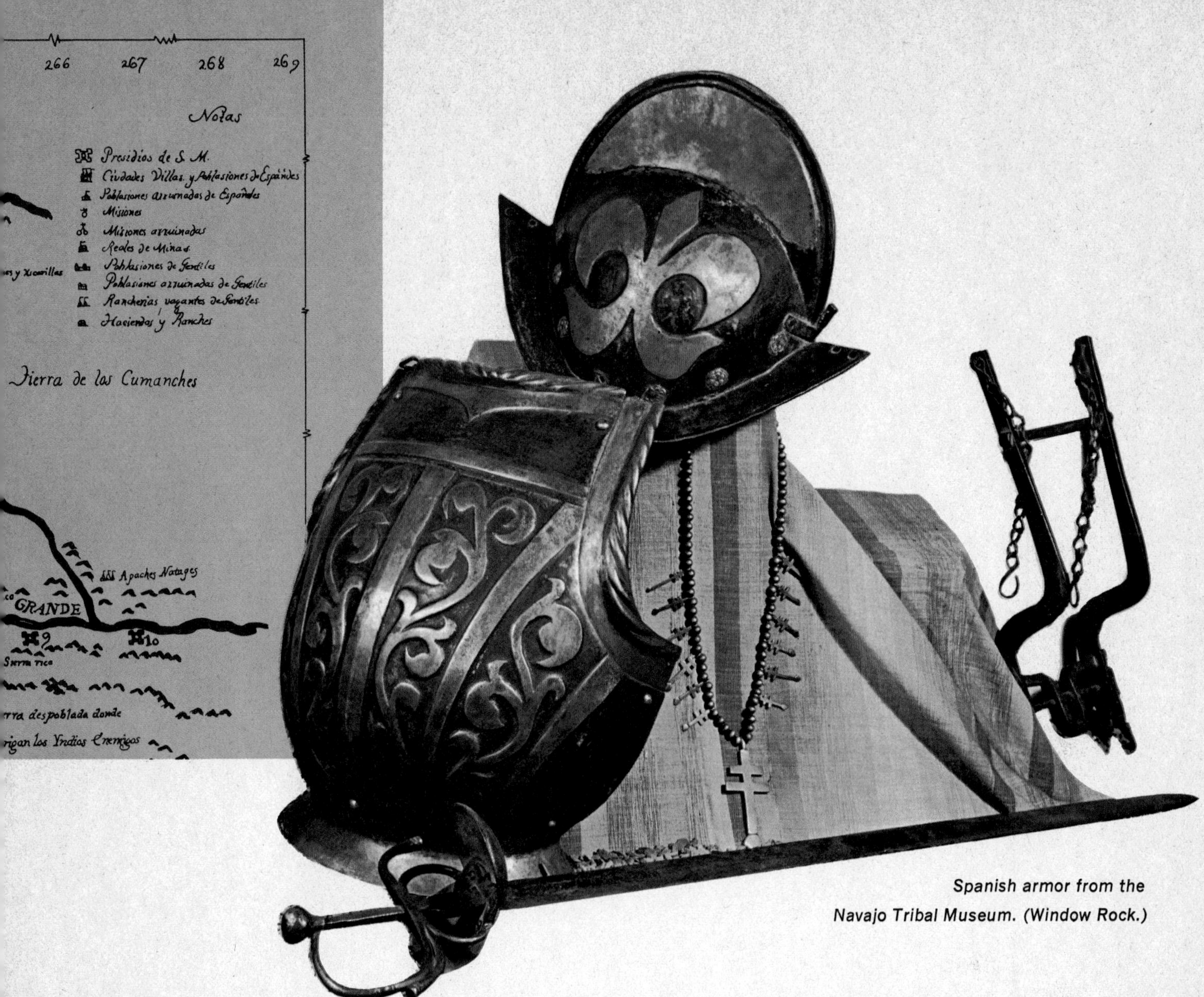

Spanish armor from the Navajo Tribal Museum. (Window Rock.)

of government and the cacique or priest-chief continued to function as the real head of the village.

Life under Spanish authority became increasingly oppressive; taxation, forced labor, and suppression of native religion resulted in the Pueblo Revolt of 1680. The tribes united in an unprecedented effort to drive out the invaders. The uprising was a success; the Spaniards retreated to El Paso and for the next twelve years the Indians once again ruled their villages. In 1693 Diego de Vargas reconquered the Indians and re-established Spanish authority in New Mexico.

Under Spanish rule the number of pueblos in the Rio Grande valley decreased from sixty-six in 1540 to nineteen in 1700. The native population was reduced by one-half.

The War of Independence transferred jurisdiction of New Mexico from Spain to Mexico in 1821. Mexico, unlike Spain, bestowed full rights of citizenship upon the Indians.

The Treaty of Guadalupe Hidalgo in 1848 marked the end of the war between the United States and Mexico, and New Mexico became a territory of the U.S. Much Indian land was lost to the new flood of settlers.

In 1849 jurisdiction over Indians was transferred from the War Department to the Bureau of Indian Affairs under the Department of the Interior where it remains today.

Despite considerable dissatisfaction with the Bureau of Indian Affairs—whose policies must necessarily change to reflect the philosophies (if any) of the political party in power—no Indian tribe in the U.S. has yet asked to be placed under the jurisdiction of a state government.

SUGGESTED READING

Hackett, Charles W. *Revolt of the Pueblo Indians of New Mexico*, U. of N.M. Press, 1942.

Kubler, George. *The Religious Architecture of New Mexico.* Taylor Museum. Colorado Springs, 1940.

Spicer, Edward H. *Cycles of Conquest*, U. of Arizona Press. Tucson, 1962. (a comprehensive study of Southwestern Indians from the time of Spanish contact to the present day).

Twitchell, Ralph E. *The Leading Facts of New Mexican History.* 2 Vol. Horn and Wallace, Pub. Albuquerque, 1963.

Rio Grande Pueblos Today

Pueblo Indian life is based on the fundamental religious conviction that man must live in harmony with the natural world about him. So strong is this belief that it is not possible to separate religion from the everyday life of the pueblos. The dances and ceremonies that are performed throughout the year are enactments of this philosophy.

Societies, headed by priests, within each pueblo are responsible for maintaining harmony with the supernatural world. Properly conducted ceremonies will control the weather, effect cures, bring rain, mature crops, and insure success in hunting.

Harmony within the pueblo must also be maintained; family, clan, and society relationships require specific behavior of the individual, and children are reared to accept these responsibilities. In such a tightly-knit society it is not surprising to find that the welfare of the group ranks before that of the individual.

Each Tewa-speaking pueblo is divided into two groups or moieties known as the Winter People and Summer People or the Squash and Turquoise. Each moiety, under the leadership of a cacique, has its own kiva or ceremonial chambers and directs the ceremonial life of the village for half of the year. Keresan-speaking pueblos have only one cacique who is responsible for the spiritual well-being of the entire pueblo. Ordinarily it is he who selects the officers to handle secular affairs. Each pueblo is politically autonomous.

Although the Catholic Church has claimed converts among the Rio Grande pueblos for over 300 years and most of the Indians make use of some services provided by the church (baptism, confirmation, marriage, burial) the importance of native religion has not diminished. The two religious systems are separate and the Indians find nothing inconsistent in making use of both.

In recent years there has been a revival in the native religion; old ceremonies have been revived and the young people have shown increased interest in participating in the ceremonial life of the pueblo.

Problems which face the pueblos are serious and numerous. Increased intermarriage with non-Indians tends to weaken pueblo authority. Population increases render present land resources inadequate. Outmoded and inequitable systems of land inheritance have fractionalized holdings until they have become impractical to farm. Agriculture, once the economic foundation of pueblo life, has become less and less important. Unemployment and underemployment are conditions that affect all age groups, but particularly the young people.

MARK BAHTI

The ancient system of choosing only old men to serve as officers and council members alienates the young educated people and deprives the pueblo of their knowledge in working with the steadily encroaching non-Indian world. Internal frictions, factionalism, and alcoholism, all symptoms of a native culture in the process of social change under pressure, weaken tribal solidarity.

A strong love for the tribal lands, a common language, and a deep attachment to the religious life of the village seem to hold the pueblo people together in the face of these difficulties.

Life in the pueblos is neither ideal nor idyllic, but it obviously holds a greater attraction and greater satisfaction for these people than an existence in the mainstream of American life.

TOURIST DIVISION NEW MEXICO DEPARTMENT OF DEVELOPMENT

HARVEY CAPLIN

Church at Acoma Pueblo (left) predates the Rebellion of 1680.

Deer dance (top) at Santa Clara Pueblo.

Grinding corn with ***mano*** *and* ***metate*** *(bottom) is a never-ending chore for the women but songs and gossip make the time pass more quickly.*

These Indian tribes have not only survived four hundred years of occupation by alien cultures but have managed to retain more of their native life than they have lost. It is probably not overly optimistic to believe that they can continue in the same manner.

SUGGESTED READING

Aberle, S.D. The Pueblo Indians of New Mexico: Their Land and Civil Organization. *American Anthropological Assn. Memoir* No. 70. 1948.

Dozier, Edward. *The Pueblo Indian of North America.* Holt, Rinehart and Winston, N. Y. 1968.

Parsons, Elsie C. *Pueblo Indian Religion.* 2 Vol. U. of Chicago Press. Chicago, 1939.

Roediger, Virginia M. *Ceremonial Costumes of the Pueblo Indians.* U. of California Press. Berkeley, 1941.

Smith, Anne M. *New Mexico Indians.* Mus. of New Mexico Research Records No. 1. Santa Fe, 1966. (an excellent summary of economic and social problems of New Mexico's tribes).

Stubbs, Stanley A. *Bird's-Eye View of the Pueblos.* U. of Okla. Press. Norman, 1950.

ACOMA ***(ah'-ko-mah) - from the native word Akome meaning "people of the white rock". Native name for the village is Ako.*** **Language - Keresan. Reservation -** ***248,200 acres.*** **Population -** ***2,420; resident - 1,680.*** **Government -** ***cacique chooses secular officers and council members.*** **Dances: Sept. 2 -** ***Harvest Dance and fiesta. Dec. 24 - Christmas Eve dance.***

Acoma, the Southwest's "Sky City" is located on top of a mesa that stands 365 feet above the surrounding valley. Acoma vies with the Hopi pueblo of Oraibi for the claim to being "the oldest continuously inhabited community in the U.S." Archaeological evidence indicates that the site has been occupied for the past thousand years.

The first European to visit the pueblo was Captain Hernando de Alvarado who arrived in 1540. At that time the Acomas, who numbered about 5,000, occupied several villages in the area.

The Spaniards feared Acoma's military potential and its control over neighboring pueblos. In 1598 Onate sent a detachment of soldiers under Juan de Zaldivar to demand tribute and supplies from the Acomas. They were attacked by the Indians who killed a number of the soldiers including Zaldivar and drove off the rest.

A punitive expedition under the command of Zaldivar's brother, Vincente, attacked the pueblo in 1599. During the three day battle which followed, hundreds of Indians were killed and the town destroyed. The captives were taken to Santo Domingo to stand trial; women over 12 years of age were sentenced to twenty years labor; men over 25 received the same fate in addition to having one foot chopped off. Young girls were given to the Church and the boys were given to Zaldivar as a reward for his victory.

In 1629 the Franciscans established the mission of San Estevan at the pueblo under the direction of Fray Ramirez. This impressive structure, which has been rebuilt and remodeled many times, loses some of its charm when it is remembered that it was originally built (like most church buildings at Indian pueblos) with forced labor.

Acoma participated in the Pueblo Revolt and later served as a refuge from the Spaniards for other Indians. In an attempt to subjugate the Acomas, De Vargas attacked their village in 1696 and laid waste their fields. Three years later

Aerial view of Acoma Pueblo. In the background is Enchanted Mesa.

DICK KENT

Acoma crafts: pottery, kachina dolls, and embroidery.

Acoma submitted to Spanish authority under Governor Cubero.

Only a few families live in the mesa top village the year round. Most occupy the permanent farming communities of Acomita and McCarthy's. All of them, however, return to the main pueblo for ceremonies.

Farming and stock raising, once the main occupations of these people, are now of secondary importance to wage work.

The best known craft of Acoma pueblo is pottery making. Many potters still produce large quantities of the carefully decorated, thin-walled ware. In addition to the traditional jars and bowl forms, copies of prehistoric vessels and figurines of animals, birds, and humans are made. Unfortunately, in recent years some of the clay used by the potters contains impurities which cause a pocking or spalling of the surface when the finished pottery absorbs moisture.

Visitors to Acoma are charged a one dollar admission fee (this includes a guide). Additional fees are charged for picture taking.

Rain trapped in catchment basins on top of the mesa formerly provided the pueblo with much of its water supply.

MARK BAHTI

SUGGESTED READING

White, Leslie A. "The Acoma Indians". *Annual Report*, Bureau of American Ethnology, No. 47. Washington, D.C. 1932.

ISLETA — *(iss-lāy'-tāh)* — ***from the Spanish word for "little island". Native name is <u>Tuei</u> meaning "town".*** **Language** - *Tiwa.* **Reservation** - *210,445 acres.* **Population** - *2,235; resident - 1,980.* **Government** - *constitution adopted in 1947. Adult male members annually elect governor, president and vice-president of council. These officers then select council members and minor officials.* **Dances:** *Aug. 28 - Corn Dance and fiesta. Dec. 24 - Christmas Eve dance.*

Area-wise Isleta is the largest of all Southwestern pueblos. It ranks second in population if one includes the "suburbs" of Chicale and the Laguna colony called Oraibi. It is not certain whether the present village occupies the same site described by the Spanish in 1540 or was founded as a new village in the early 1700's.

The population of Isleta was greatly increased in the 1600's by an influx of refugees from other Tiwa villages who sought protection from Apache raids. In 1680 the population was estimated to be 2,000. Of the twenty villages which comprised the Southern Tiwa province at the time of Spanish contact only Isleta remained by the late 1700's.

The large numbers of Spanish settlers who moved to Isleta prior to the 1680 revolt unwittingly prevented that village from taking part in the initial uprising. Before Gov. Otermin reached Isleta on his retreat to El Paso, however, most of the villagers had abandoned their pueblo and joined the insurgents.

In 1681, Governor Otermin, during his unsuccessful attempt to reconquer New Mexico, attacked several Southern Tiwa villages including Isleta. He took hundreds of captives whom he settled south of El Paso at a new village called Isleta del Sur. Descendents of this group still live there but have lost much of their cultural identity.

Isleta was the only Rio Grande pueblo to adopt the Spanish custom of electing a governor. This caused a certain amount of confusion in leadership since it usurped the power of the cacique who ordinarily selected secular officials. By 1880 serious factionalism developed over this issue, and the dissent over leadership in village affairs and election procedures continues to this day. A constitution and council form of government, adopted in 1947, has not yet succeeded in solving the problems.

Agriculture as a community enterprise is being tried at Isleta with some success. Many people, however, still maintain their own garden plots and raise stock. Wage work in nearby Albuquerque is probably the most important single source of income. Some craft work, silversmithing and weaving, is still produced but in decreasing amounts. The so-called Isleta pottery is made by the Laguna colony which settled at Isleta in 1880.

Despite its factionalism Isleta maintains a full and active ceremonial life.

The church of San Antonio de la Isleta has been rebuilt and remodeled a number of times but probably includes portions of the original mission of San Agustin de la Isleta built in 1626.

SUGGESTED READING

French, David H. *Factionalism in Isleta Pueblo.* Amercan Ethnological Society. Monograph 14. New York, 1948.

Parsons, Elsie C. "Isleta, New Mexico", *U.S. Bureau of American Ethnology,* No. 47, Wash. D.C. 1932.

The church of San Antonio de la Isleta includes portions of the original 17th Century structure.

MARK BAHTI

JEMEZ *(hay'-mess)* — ***Spanish spelling of the native name Hemis meaning "Hemis people". Native name for the pueblo is Walatowa which means "the people in the canyon".*** **Language** - *Towa.* **Reservation** - *86,696 acres.* **Population** - *1,570; resident - 1,080.* **Government** - *cacique selects secular officers. Tribal council composed of former governors.* **Dances:** *June 24 - San Juan's Day celebration. Aug. 2 - Old Pecos Bull Dance. Nov. 12 - Harvest Dance and fiesta.*

Jemez pottery and plaited yucca basket.

This Towa-speaking tribe inhabited a number of villages on the tributaries of the Jemez River before moving into the main Jemez Valley. At the time of Spanish contact in 1541 they were living in eleven small villages in the Agua Caliente region.

In accordance with the Spanish policy of consolidating Indian populations wherever possible, the Jemez people were persuaded to abandon most of their pueblos so that by 1625 they were concentrated in only two villages. In each of these the Spaniards established missions.

From their earliest contacts the tribe maintained a hostile attitude toward the Spanish. Two unsuccessful uprisings against Spanish authority occurred at Jemez before the Pueblo Rebellion of 1680.

Spanish efforts to reconquer Jemez were thwarted by the villagers who retreated to fortified positions on the nearby mesa whenever soldiers appeared. From this stronghold they sent out raiding parties to harass Santa Ana and Zia for remaining loyal to the Spaniards.

In 1694 De Vargas, with the help of Indian allies from Santa Ana, Zia and San Felipe, attacked and destroyed their mesa village and the survivors of this battle resettled Giusewa, one of their villages in the valley.

Before long, however, the Jemez had enlisted military aid from the Zuni, Acoma, and Navajo tribes and resumed their hostilities against the pueblos to the south. The Jemez Rebellion was finally crushed and those who escaped found refuge among the Navajo and the Hopi. (The Hemis kachina, a popular figure at Niman dances, was introduced to the Hopi by the Jemez people at that time.)

In 1703 most of the people returned to the Jemez Valley and built their present village at the site of an earlier settlement. In 1836 they were joined by the remaining inhabitants of Pecos, a Towa-speaking pueblo in the Galisteo Basin.

Although many families farm small garden plots, agriculture is becoming less important to the pueblo's economy. Cattle raising and seasonal wage work provide some income. Unemployment is high at Jemez because of its distance from urban areas.

Plaited, bowl-shaped baskets of yucca, pottery (mostly of the garish poster paint variety) and fine embroidery are the crafts presently produced at the pueblo.

SUGGESTED READING

White, Leslie A. *The Pueblo of Jemez.* Phillips Academy. Andover, 1925.

HARVEY CAPLIN

*Making **piki** requires a light touch; this paper-thin cornbread is made by smearing a flour and water mixture over a hot stone griddle with the bare hand.*

COCHITI (kō'-chĭ-tee) — *Spanish version of native name Kotyete of unknown meaning.* **Language** - *Keresan.* **Reservation** - *26,491 acres.* **Population** - *655; resident - 390.* **Government** - *religious hierarchy selects secular officers annually; council made up of former officers.* **Dances:** *June 13 - San Antonio's Day dance. June 24 - San Juan's Day celebration. July 14 - Corn Dance and fiesta.*

Before the arrival of the Spanish, the people of Cochiti and San Felipe had formed a single tribe. Warfare with their Tewa neighbors caused a split, and the two groups established separate villages in 1250 A.D. The present pueblo of Cochiti dates from this period.

Onate visited Cochiti in 1598. The mission of San Buenaventura was built there in 1628. Although it was rebuilt in the 18th century and has been extensively remodeled many times, the present church at the pueblo contains sections of the original structure.

The Cochitis abandoned their pueblo after the 1680 Rebellion and retreated to the fortified village of Cieneguilla with Indians from Santo Domingo, Taos, San Felipe, and Picuris .

In 1692 this band of insurgents promised De Vargas to return to its villages peacefully. Only San Felipe kept its word; the others decided to continue their resistance. Under cover of darkness, De Vargas's soldiers and their Indian allies attacked the rebels, destroyed the village, and took many prisoners. Cochiti was not resettled until 1694.

During the late 1700's and early 1800's, Cochiti served as a refuge for Spanish and Mexican colonists from Navajo and Apache raids. As a result of this early contact there has been considerable intermarriage between the two groups. Even today a few Spanish-American families still live in the pueblo.

Conservative and progressive groups are present in Cochiti with control of village affairs in the hands of the conservatives, but serious factionalism has been avoided and progressive members have been urged to participate in council discussions even though they do not take part in ceremonial affairs. Cochiti maintains a full ceremonial calendar which includes a number of kachina dances not open to the public.

Until recently agriculture was the important economic activity at Cochiti. Farming is now limited to garden plots and alfalfa. The completion of nearby Cochiti Dam may provide new economic opportunities that could benefit the pueblo.

Drums and pottery are the best known Cochiti crafts. Cochiti drums, noted for their superior workmanship and fine tone, are very popular with other Indians.

The tourist as seen by a Cochiti potter.

A master Cochiti drum maker.

SUGGESTED READING

Lange, Charles. *Cochiti.* U. of Texas Press. Austin, 1959.

PHOTOGRAPHS BY K. C. DEN DOOVEN

Cochiti drums are made from hollowed out cottonwood logs and horsehide; tone varies with size and shape.

TAOS *(täh'-ōs)* — *from the Spanish version of the native name* *Tua* *meaning "houses" or "village".* **Language** - *Tiwa.* **Reservation** - *47,334 acres.* **Population** - *1,500; resident - 900.* **Government** - *religious hierarchy made up of four kiva headmen and hereditary cacique select secular officers.* **Dances:** *Jan. 1 - Turtle Dance. Jan. 6 - Animal Dance. June 13 - Corn Dance. July 25 - Corn Dance. Sept. 29 - Sundown Dance. Sept. 30 - fiesta. Dec. 24 - Christmas Eve procession. Dec. 25 - Matachines Dance. (Check dates locally).*

The northernmost pueblo, Taos, shows the influence of Plains tribes in the dress, customs and physical makeup of its people. The Ute, Apache and Comanche met here to trade meat and hides for pueblo foodstuffs and textiles. The multistoried construction of the pueblo, designed for defense, and the surrounding adobe wall give evidence that not all contacts were peaceful.

The present village was built about 1700 after the old one, located a few hundred yards to the northeast, was destroyed by fire in the 1690's. It closely duplicates the original pueblo, consisting of two house groups: Hlauuma (North House) and Hlaukwima (South House) located on either side of Taos Creek.

Alvarado first visited Taos in 1540. In 1598 Onate, following the Spanish custom of assigning saints' names to Indian pueblos, named it San Miguel. No trace remains of the original mission of San Geronimo established in the early 17th Century. The church ruins (also called San Geronimo) inside the wall date from 1706. The present church was built in 1847.

Dissatisfaction with Spanish rule led to the abandonment of the village in 1639 and the people moved onto the plains with the Jicarilla Apaches. They built a new pueblo in what is now Scott County, Kansas, and remained there for two years before they were brought back to Taos by the Spaniards.

Trouble with Spanish authority continued and Taos served as the base of operation for the conspirators who planned the Pueblo Rebellion of 1680. On August tenth of that year Taos warriors killed the resident priests and Spanish settlers and joined the other pueblos in attacking Santa Fe. The move was a military success and Governor Otermin was forced to retreat south to El Paso with all Spanish colonists.

In 1692 the Spaniards under De Vargas succeded in reconquering the province. An uneasy truce followed, marked by minor revolts and temporary abandonments of Taos when the people fled to nearby mountain canyons to escape Spanish reprisals.

The only major uprising at Taos after the U.S. assumed control of the territory occurred in 1847. The Taos Rebellion, instigated by Mexicans who harbored ill-feelings toward the American

---

PICURIS *(pee-kū-reece')* — *probably a Spanish version of the Keresan name* *Pikuria.* *Native name is* *Piwwetha* *meaning "pass in the mountains".* **Language** - *Tiwa.* **Reservation** - *14,959 acres.* **Population** - *285; resident - 100.* **Government** - *religious hierarchy chooses secular officers.* **Dances:** *Aug. 10 - fiesta and Corn Dance.*

Picuris and Taos are descended from a common ancestral group which settled in the present general area about 900 A.D. Sometime during the 12th century, these people split to form two separate tribes. Picuris, like Taos, has had considerable contact with Plains tribes and particularly the Jicarilla Apaches with whom they frequently intermarried.

The original pueblo, now partially excavated, lies on the north edge of the present village. It dates from about 1250 A.D. and was visited by the Spaniards in the early 1540's. They named the village San Lorenzo and established a mission there in 1621.

Luis Tupato, one of the leaders of the Pueblo Revolt, was the governor of Picuris. The pueblo, which at that time had a population of 3,000, played an important role in the rebellion by providing a large force of fighting men for the campaign against the Spanish.

MARK BAHTI

The ruins of Old Picuris have been excavated as a tourist attraction.

conquerors, resulted in the death of Governor Charles Bent and seven Americans. Troops from Santa Fe attacked and killed 150 rebels who sought refuge in the church (the ruins of which are still visible inside the wall) and later executed fifteen.

Encroachment on pueblo land by white squatters led to a threatened uprising in 1910 but the appearance of troops prevented bloodshed.

Hlaukwima– South House – of Taos Pueblo.

HARVEY CAPLIN

Problems at Taos are not all related to outside influences; factionalism within the pueblo is a common condition. The introduction of the peyote cult in the 1890's resulted in fifty years of bitter conflict.

The control of village affairs in the hands of a conservative religious hierarchy, lack of land, and limited job opportunities have led to frustration among the younger members of the pueblo. Politically powerless and economically insecure, many of them have left Taos to seek employment elsewhere. Internal dissension has prevented the development of economic opportunities necessary to meet the needs of a growing population.

Nevertheless, Taos continues to function as a pueblo society held together by the strong ties of a common language, culture and religion.

SUGGESTED READING

Fenton, William N. *Factionalism at Taos Pueblo New Mexico.* Bureau of American Ethnology, Bulletin No. 164. Washington, 1957.

Parsons, Elsie Clews. *Taos Pueblo.* General Series in Anthropology, No. 2 Menasha, 1936.

Picuris bean pots.

In 1692 they once again swore allegiance to Spanish authority but followed this with three more revolts in less than five years. After the last uprising in 1696, they abandond their village to seek refuge at the Jicarilla Apache settlement of El Cuartelejo in western Kansas. In 1706, greatly decimated by disease and warfare, they returned to their pueblo. The present church was built in the 1770's following the resettlement of the village.

At the present time Picuris is in a state of cultural disintegration. Lack of local employment forces those with skills or education to leave the pueblo thereby depriving the village of the leadership it needs to develop into a self-sufficient community. There is a lack of tribal unity, and secular leaders lack community support. Those who live at the pueblo supplement their seasonal wage work incomes with subsistence farming, cattle raising, and craftwork.

Picuris pottery, made from a mica-flecked clay, has been traded widely for hundreds of years. Half a dozen women still produce this undecorated cooking ware which is much sought after by both Indians and Anglos. It is one of the few types of pueblo pottery that still serves a utilitarian purpose.

San Juan pottery and carved deer dancer figures.

SAN JUAN *(săn - hwăn) — Spanish for Saint John. Native name is Oke - meaning unknown.* **Language** *- Tewa.* **Reservation** *- 12,331 acres.* **Population** *- 1,260; resident - 700.* **Government** *- religious leaders of winter and summer people alternate in annual selection of secular officers. Council made up of all former governors.* **Dances:** *June 24 - fiesta and Corn Dance.*

San Juan, the largest of the Tewa-speaking pueblos, has been continuously inhabited since 1300 A.D.

In 1598 Onate established the first capital of New Mexico at this village. The following year the Spaniards moved their headquarters across the river to the village of Yunqueyunque ("village of the ravine"). The inhabitants of Yunqueyunque who relinquished their pueblo to the Spanish took up residence in San Juan. The hospitality of San Juan in receiving these people so impressed the Spaniards that they bestowed the name of "San Juan de los Caballeros" on the pueblo.

This initial period of good will soon gave way to feelings of discontent and hostility as the Indians experienced the harshness of Spanish rule. Suppression of native religion reached a peak in 1675 when forty-seven Indian leaders from a number of pueblos were convicted of practicing witchcraft and whipped. Among them was Pope', a medicine man from San Juan, who later conceived, organized, and led the Pueblo Rebellion of 1680 which drove the Spanish colonists from the Rio Grande valley. This was the only time the pueblos had ever united to achieve a common goal.

Pope' then attempted to purge the country of all Spanish influence and to return the pueblos to the old way of life, but he became so tyrannical in his methods that he soon lost the support of the people; the pueblos withdrew to their own village authorities and the spirit of inter-tribal cooperation disappeared. This lack of unity worked to the advantage of De Vargas during his reconquest of New Mexico.

Today San Juan is in a state of transition and beset by many internal problems. One half of the population has left the pueblo to find employment in urban centers. Those who remain engage in farming and find part-time or seasonal jobs as agricultural workers. There are almost no job opportunities at the pueblo for educated young people; neither do they have a voice in village affairs for secular officials are appointed by religious leaders and not elected. As a result the appointed officers get little support from the villagers.

Despite this friction there has been an increase in the ceremonial activities of the pueblo and a number of rituals have been revived. There has also been a revival of arts and crafts in San Juan; woodcarvings of dance figures, embroidery and basketry are now being produced in addition to increased quantities of pottery.

SANDIA *(sähn-dee'-yah)* — ***Spanish word for watermelon. Native name is Nafiat meaning "a dusty or sandy place".*** **Language** - *Tiwa.* **Reservation** - *22,883 acres.* **Population** - *240; resident - 125.* **Government** - *cacique appoints secular officers.* **Dances:** *June 13 - Corn Dance and fiesta. Dec 31 - New Year's Eve Deer Dance.*

The Pueblo of Sandia dates from about 1300 A.D. Remains of the early village visited by Coronado in 1540 are still visible near the present church.

In the early 17th century the Franciscans built the mission of San Francisco at the village. It was destroyed during the Rebellion in 1680. (The existing church was built in the early 1890's).

In fear of Spanish reprisals the Sandia people abandoned their pueblo after the rebellion and took refuge with the Hopis. On Second Mesa, north of the pueblo of Mishongnovi, they established the village of Payupki where they lived until 1742 when Padres Delgado and Pino persuaded about 500 of them to return to New Mexico. They re-established their village on the site of the old one (destroyed by Gov. Otermin during his attempt at reconquest in 1681). The new pueblo was named Nuestra Senora de los Dolores y San Antonio de Sandia; the Hopis call it Payupki.

In spite of its proximity to Albuquerque little is known about Sandia and it maintains an air of secrecy about its ceremonial life.

The secular officers of the pueblo, usually able young men, are appointed by the cacique who is the head of a hierarchy of priests.

Wage work in nearby towns and farming provide the economic base for this pueblo. No craftwork is being produced currently. Sandia's future as an Indian village is in doubt since it lies in the path of the ever-expanding city of Albuquerque. Pressures to change will increase as the geographical isolation of the pueblo decreases.

A ***manta*** *— the original basic black dress of the pueblo woman — is often combined today with a cotton dress, shawl, and lace apron.*

SAN FELIPE *(săn fay-lee'-pay)* — *Spanish name for Saint Philip. Native name is Katishtya - meaning unknown.* **Language** - *Keresan.* **Reservation** - *48,930 acres.* **Population** - *1,350; resident - 1,060.* **Government** - *religious leader selects secular officers and council.* **Dances:** *Feb. 2 - Buffalo Dance. May 1 - fiesta and Corn Dance. June 29 - San Pedro's Day celebration. Dec. 24 - Christmas Eve dance.*

The present pueblo, which dates from the early 1700's, is the fourth village to bear the native name of Katishtya. The first, located farther south, was abandoned before the Spaniards arrived. The second, named San Felipe by Castana de Sosa in 1591, was on the east bank of the Rio Grande at the foot of Tamita Mesa. Here, in the early 1600's, a mission was established and maintained until the Rebellion of 1680 when the villagers destroyed the church and abandoned their pueblo.

Fearful of Spanish reprisals, the San Felipans joined forces with refugees from several other pueblos at Cieneguilla, a fortified site north of Cochiti.

In 1693 General de Vargas persuaded the San Felipans to leave their fortress. The third village of Katishtya was then established in a defensive position on the top of Black Mesa on the west side of the Rio Grande. San Felipe remained obedient to the Spanish thereafter and provided warriors to aid the Spaniards in subduing other pueblo tribes. This village was abandoned in 1700 and the present town built at the foot of the mesa. The present church dates from 1706.

San Felipe shares with Santo Domingo a reputation for being a very conservative village. One cacique, the religious leader of the village, appoints all secular officers and council members. This form of government precludes elections and limits participation in village affairs by its younger members. The number of young people who leave the pueblo to seek outside employment has risen steadily in recent years.

Farming, which has declined in importance as an economic pursuit, may improve if present plans for land and water distribution are carried out.

San Felipe has always been noted among the Rio Grande pueblos for its beautiful ceremonial dances, and in recent years a number of old rituals have been revived.

Except for a recent—and not too successful—attempt to revive pottery making, no crafts are produced at this village.

SUGGESTED READING

White, Leslie A. *The Pueblo of San Felipe.* American Anthropological Assn. Menasha, 1932.

San Felipe Pueblo is located between the Rio Grande and the foot of Black Mesa.

LAURA GILPIN

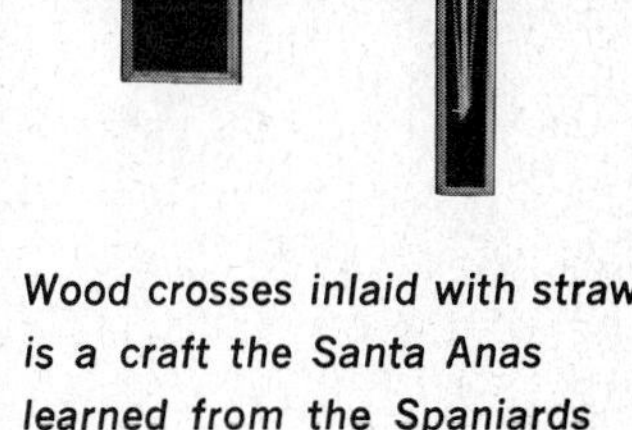

Wood crosses inlaid with straw is a craft the Santa Anas learned from the Spaniards

The church at Santa Ana Pueblo was rebuilt in 1734.

SANTA ANA *(sän'-ta ăn-ä)* — *Spanish name for Saint Anne. Native name is Tamaya - meaning unknown.* **Language** - *Keresan.* **Reservation** - *19,106 acres.* **Population** - *435; resident - 370.* **Government** - *cacique selects secular officers annually. Council includes all adult male family heads.* **Dances:** *July 26 - Green Corn Dance and fiesta.*

A lack of agricultural land and water for irrigation has forced the virtual abandonment of the pueblo of Santa Ana. Most of the tribe now lives at Ranchos de Santa Ana, a farming community on the Rio Grande near Bernalillo. Only a few people remain behind to take care of the pueblo.

Santa Ana remains active ceremonially and the people return to their village to perform their dances. At all other times the pueblo remains closed to visitors.

Onate visited Tamaja, which he renamed Santa Ana, in 1598 and a mission was built there in the 17th century. In 1680 Santa Ana, San Felipe, and Santo Domingo joined forces to drive the Spanish settlers from their territory.

Pedro de Posada, the governor of El Paso, led an attack on Santa Ana in 1687 and burned the village. Those who escaped united with survivors from Zia to establish a village on Red Mesa near Jemez as a defense against the Spanish. In 1692 De Vargas persuaded them to return to Santa Ana and rebuild the village. After this they remained loyal to Spanish rule; for this they suffered periodic raids by the Jemez people who wanted all pueblos to continue to resist the Spaniards.

The present church at Santa Ana dates from 1734 but may include portions of the earlier mission.

As the result of a revival in the 1940's pottery is still being made at Santa Ana but in very limited amounts. Crosses of wood, inlaid with straw (a folk art adopted from the Spaniards) and small, painted wood carvings of animals are also produced.

SUGGESTED READING

White, Leslie A. *The Pueblo of Santa Ana, New Mexico.* American Anthropological Assn. Memoir No. 60, 1942

HARVEY CAPLIN

The influence of Indian artists found on the facade of the church at Santo Domingo is not seen in earlier missions.

SANTO DOMINGO *(sän'-to dō-ming'-gō)*

— Spanish name for Saint Dominic. Native name is <u>Kiuwa</u> - meaning unknown.* Language - *Keresan.* Reservation - *66,231 acres.* Population - *1,980; resident - 1,940.* Government - *council made up of former governors chooses secular officers annually. Strong control over village government by religious leaders.* Dances: *June 29 - San Pedro's Day celebration. Aug. 4 - Corn Dance and fiesta. Dec. 24 - Christmas Eve dance.

Santo Domingo has long been known as the most conservative of all the pueblos and nothing has been done thus far which would indicate it is about to give up the title. The people are friendly but independent. They maintain a high degree of tribal unity in governmental and religious affairs despite outside pressures to change.

The present pueblo of Santo Domingo dates from about 1700. A disastrous flood in 1886 destroyed much of the town and its church. It was soon rebuilt and a new church (the present one) constructed in 1890. Floods have always been a particular menace to the villagers; at least three of their earlier towns and two Spanish missions have been destroyed by Rio Grande floodwaters.

Onate visited Santo Domingo in 1598 and met there with the leaders of more than thirty pueblos. Whether they fully understood that the Spaniards were claiming their land is not known, but Onate accepted the idea that he had received pledges of allegiance to both the Crown and the Church from all those assembled.

Alonza Catiti, an interpreter from Santo Domingo, was one of the three leaders of the Pueblo Rebellion of 1680. The village was abandoned at that time and the people moved to La Cieneguilla in anticipation of a Spanish attack. In 1683 most of them returned to their village.

The Santo Domingans resisted reconquest by the Spaniards; they destroyed their pueblo in 1692 and joined forces with the Indians of Jemez. Their village near Jemez was destroyed by De Vargas two years later and many of the people were taken captive. Some who escaped fled to the Hopi villages, and others who had remained with the rebels at Cieneguilla moved to Acoma country with some Cochiti refugees where they established the new pueblo of Laguna.

Santo Domingo was later resettled by De Vargas's captives and those who returned from Hopi country. A number of Tanos Indians from the Galisteo Basin — refugees from Comanche raids — also joined the pueblo.

As far as was possible the people followed a policy of passive resistance toward the Spanish. Native ceremonies were carried on in secrecy in defiance to the Catholic church. Their present dislike for those who would pry into native rituals is probably a direct carry-over from those times.

Electricity, plumbing, and other modern conveniences are much in evidence at the pueblo, but

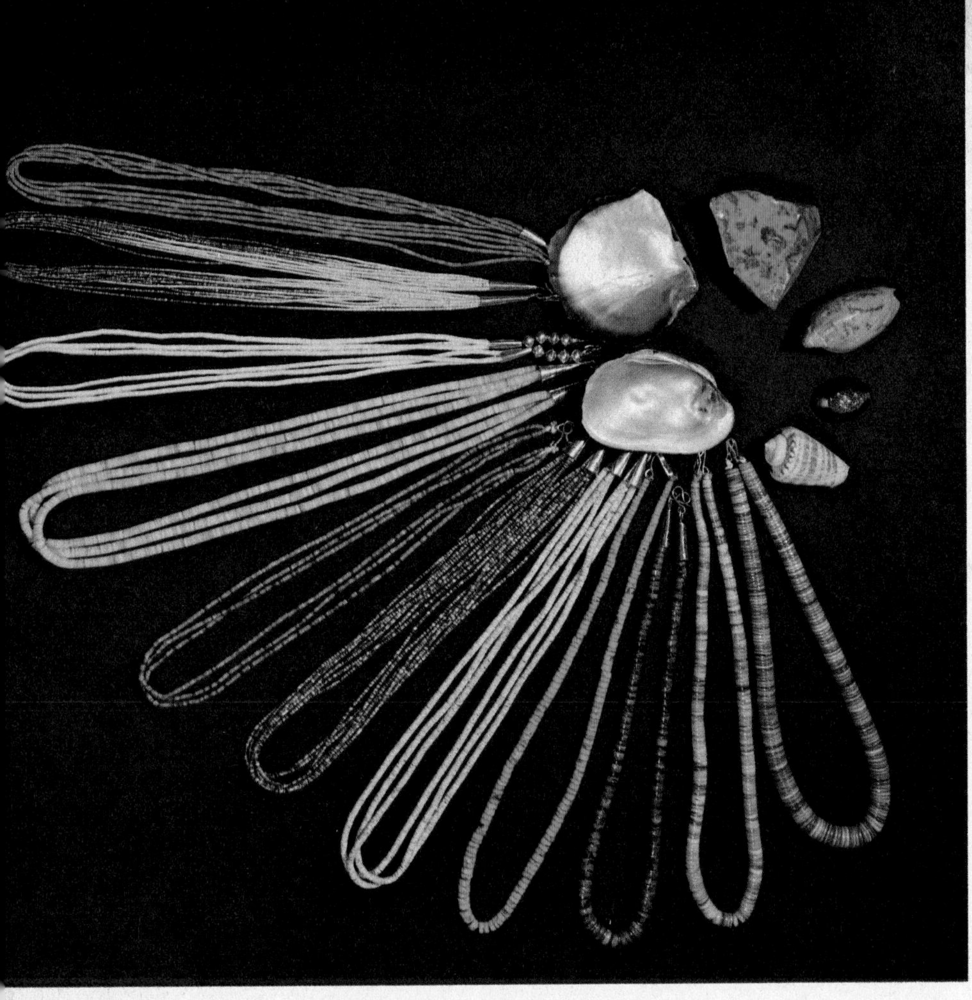

Santo Domingo bead makers use turquoise and a wide variety of sea shells in creating necklaces.

ANTHROPOLOGY MUSEUM-U.N.M.

***Koshares,** sacred clowns, alleviate the solemnity of ceremonials with their antics.*

the people resist any change that would alter their way of life. Only recently, for example, have they expressed a desire for better schooling for their children.

The economy of the pueblo is based on subsistence farming, cattle raising, wage work, and fire fighting. Local resources will soon be inadequate to meet the needs of a rapidly increasing population.

Many villagers supplement their incomes with craftwork. Pottery and silver jewelry are produced, but they are best known for their beads of shell and turquoise. These necklaces (erroneously called wampum) are much in demand by Indians of other tribes; as a result the Santo Domingans have become itinerant salesmen. (As early as 1850 they were reported trading with tribes in Oklahoma). It is not uncommon to find these Indians selling their wares in distant cities.

It is difficult not to admire the Santo Domingans — and other Indians like them — for resisting the pressures which would change their colorful life to that uniformly gray existence of the "average citizen".

SUGGESTED READING

White, Leslie A. "The Pueblo of Santo Domingo, New Mexico". *American Anthropological Assn. Memoir No. 34,* Menasha, 1935.

TESUQUE ***(tĕh-soo'-key) — Spanish corruption of the native name Tatunge meaning "dry spotted place". Language - Tewa. Reservation - 17,024 acres. Population - 225; resident - 140. Government - religious leaders choose secular officers annually. Dances: Nov. 12 - fiesta and Harvest Dance. Dec. 24 - Christmas Eve dance.***

Tesuque has probably occupied two separate sites in historic times. Their first village was located three miles west of the present pueblo. It was abandoned and its 17th century mission destroyed during the 1680 revolt. Tesuque struck the first blow of the Pueblo Rebellion and took part in the general attack on Santa Fe; after this the villagers scattered to join other rebel Tewas at Black Mesa and La Cieneguilla and did not return to re-establish their village until the early 1700's.

The pueblo of Tesuque has kept much of its old way of life; religious and political leadership remain in the hands of two caciques, the heads of the village's Winter and Summer moieties. Nevertheless, they maintain a practical and progressive attitude by appointing young capable men to those secular offices which handle business affairs outside the pueblo.

Tesuque produced a very creditable pottery, but this disappeared in the early 1900's and the potters began to cater to the American tourist by turning out clay knick-knacks decorated with watercolor paints. The most infamous of these is the so-called Tesuque Rain God which was originally produced as a giveaway for a mid-western candy manufacturer. Probably patterned after a figurine from Old Mexico, it has no connection with Tesuque, rain, or gods. It is still being made and sold today — which goes to prove Mencken was right when he said, "No one ever lost a dime by underestimating the bad taste of the American public".

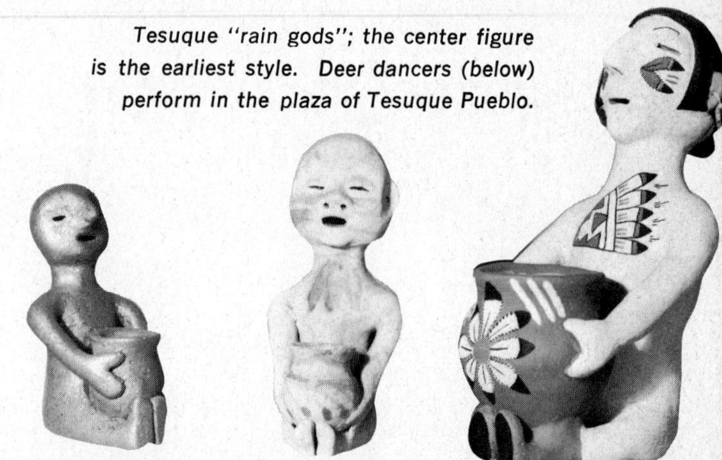

Tesuque "rain gods"; the center figure is the earliest style. Deer dancers (below) perform in the plaza of Tesuque Pueblo.

LAURA GILPIN

Zia pottery, recognized for its fine quality, has always been popular with other pueblos.

ZIA ***(tsee'-äh) — from the native name Tseja - meaning unknown.*** **Language - *Keresan.*** **Reservation - *89,035 acres.*** **Population - *470; resident - 380.*** **Government - *cacique selects governor. Governor appoints committee to handle secular affairs. Council made up of all adult males.*** **Dances: *August 15 - Corn Dance and fiesta.***

Early Spanish accounts refer to Zia as the largest (2,500 population) and most important town in a province containing five pueblos. Onate visited the village in 1598 and shortly thereafter the mission of Nuestra Senora de la Asuncion de Sia was established.

Zia took an active part in the Pueblo Rebellion and remained defiant to Spanish attempts at reconquest. In 1689 Gov. Domingo de Cruzate attacked Zia, and in a bloody battle killed more than 600 Indians, destroyed the town, and sold the captives into slavery. Those who escaped built a new pueblo near Jemez where they stayed until 1692 when De Vargas induced them to return to Zia and to rebuild the pueblo and its church. From this time on they remained friendly to the Spaniards and often served as allies in attacks on other pueblos. This loyalty to the Spanish did not endear them to the other tribes and Zia frequently found itself the target of punitive raids by neighboring pueblos. Even today the inhabitants of this village are regarded as social outcasts because of this alliance.

Because of inadequate land and water Zia has always been a poor pueblo. Limited cattle raising and farming is carried on but wage work in nearby communities accounts for most of the pueblo's income.

Internal strife is common at Zia. In the 1930's a group of Zias living in Albuquerque joined an evangelical sect of faith healers. The converts returned to the pueblo to seek new members and after much controversy returned to Albuquerque. Other factionalism resulted in the burning of a kiva belonging to a rival group.

Faced by a shortage of land, an increasing population, and continuing internal unrest the future of Zia is in doubt.

Zia potters are widely known for their fine polychrome ware which they trade to Indians and non-Indians alike. (New Mexico's state flag is derived from a Zia pottery design.)

SUGGESTED READING

Stevenson, Matilda C. "The Sia". *U.S. Bureau of American Ethnology. 11th Annual Report.* Washington, 1894

Santa Clara and San Ildefonso carved and painted pottery.

K. C DEN DOOVEN

SANTA CLARA — *Spanish for Saint Claire. Native name is Ka'po - meaning unknown.* **Language** - *Tewa.* **Reservation** - *45,742 acres.* **Population** - *910; resident - 540.* **Government** - *officers and council elected annually by adult male and female tribal members. Tribal constitution adopted in 1935.* **Dances:** *June 8 - Buffalo Dance. Aug. 12 - fiesta and Corn Dance. August - Puye Cliffs celebration.*

According to their tradition the Tewas emerged from the underworld through *Sip-ophe,* a small lake in the sand dune country near Alamosa, Colorado. Before they settled in their present locations the Tewas also claim to have occupied several villages in the Ojo Caliente area in addition to the cliff dwellings at Puye'. Santa Clara, one of six Tewa-speaking pueblos in New Mexico, was built in the 14th century.

The Spaniards established a church at the village in the 1620's. The present church, which dates from 1918, occupies the site of the original structure.

At the time of the 1680 rebellion the Santa Clarans attacked a small party of Spanish soldiers at the pueblo, fortified their village against possible attack, and joined their allies to lay siege to Santa Fe. Later they joined other Tewas in the fortress on Black Mesa. Some moved west to take up residence with the Zuni and Hopi; after the reconquest of New Mexico many moved back to reoccupy their village.

In the late 1800's Santa Clara split into opposing factions over a controversy involving the acceptance of federal programs. Those who wished to co-operate with the government were accused of abandoning the old ways, and charges of witchcraft were a common occurrence.

The adoption of a tribal constitution in 1935 has done much to heal this factionalism. Today the traditional religious hierarchy directs the ceremonial life of the village and secular affairs are left in the hands of the progressive, educated young. The arrangement has been so successful that many of the disenfranchised young people of neighboring pueblos point to Santa Clara as an example of how things *could* be if only the religious leaders of their villages would relinquish control over secular positions.

Santa Clara, like San Ildefonso, is famous for its polished black pottery. An estimated seventy-five potters produce large numbers of bowls, jars, plates, and a seemingly endless variety of figurines. Polished red ware and a red polychrome are also made.

As with most pueblos, agriculture has been superseded by wage work as the most important source of income. Many Santa Clarans are employed at Los Alamos.

Tribal income is derived from commercial properties near Espanola and the small fees charged visitors to Santa Clara Canyon and the Puye' Cliffs.

SUGGESTED READING

Parsons, Elsie C. "The Social Organization of the Tewa of New Mexico". *Amer. Anthropological Assn.* Menasha, 1929.

LAURA GILPIN

Green Corn dance at San Ildefonso Pueblo.

SAN ILDEFONSO *(săn ill-dee-fon'-sō)* —

Spanish for Saint Ildefonsus. Native name is Pokwoge meaning "where the water cuts down through". Language - Tewa. Reservation - 25,757 acres. Population - 300; resident - 225. Government - governor and council elected biennially by adult male tribal members. Dances: Jan. 6 - Eagle Dance. Jan. 23 - fiesta, Animal Dance and Comanche Dance. June 13 - Corn Dance. Sept. 8 - Harvest Dance.

According to one tradition at San Ildefonso, the cliff dwellings of Mesa Verde are the ancestral homes of this tribe. Archaeological evidence indicates that the Indians of San Ildefonso had also occupied, along with other Tewa-speaking groups, three villages on the Pajarito plateau before they settled in their present location.

They have inhabited this area from about 1300 A.D. although the actual village site has been shifted a number of times. The village which Onate visited in 1598 was located about one mile from the present pueblo.

The Spaniards established a mission at the village in 1617. It was destroyed by the Indians when they took part in the Rebellion of 1680. (The present church was built in 1905).

In seeking a site which could be more easily defended against the return of the Spaniards, the people abandoned their village in 1694 and moved to the top of nearby Black Mesa. Here, with allies from other neighboring tribes, they successfully withstood three assaults by De Vargas's troops. After holding out for nine months in this mesa top fortress they finally surrendered and returned to their village.

Crop failures and continued religious suppression led to another revolt against Spanish authority in 1696. Most of the people abandoned the pueblo and sought refuge among other tribes; some moved as far west as the Hopi villages and took up residence there. In 1702 the Spanish resettled San Ildefonso with other Tewa-speaking people.

Trouble continued to plague the village. In the late 1700's an estimated one-half of the population was wiped out by a smallpox epidemic. Religious suppression continued, and San Ildefonso was the scene of a number of witchcraft trials.

In 1910, in an attempt to avert further misfortunes, the religious leaders of the pueblo decided to change the location of the village. About half of the people moved south around what is now known as the South Plaza; the other half refused to relocate and continued to occupy the North Plaza. This resulted in serious religious and political factionalism, for the religious leadership of the pueblo was centered in South Village and secular offices remained in North Village. This split, which wracked the pueblo for over fifty years, is now almost entirely healed and village programs reflect a cooperative community spirit.

The polished black pottery for which San Ildefonso is famous is a revival of an earlier style found in the ruins on Pajarito plateau. Experiments to reproduce this early ware were encouraged by the School of American Research in Santa Fe. So successful were these experiments that production of this pottery soon became an important source of income for the village. In 1919 Maria Martinez—the most famous of all Indian potters—and her husband Julian began to make a polished ware decorated with matte black designs. Rosalie Aguilar produced the first carved ware in 1931. A number of excellent potters continue to make fine polished black and red ware using both decorative techniques.

For anyone inclined to complain about the prices charged for San Ildefonso pottery, it is probably worth noting that as early as 1915 prices were regarded as "fantastic".

SUGGESTED READING

Marriott, Alice. *Maria: The Potter of San Ildefonso.* U. of Oklahoma Press. Norman, 1948.

Whitman, William. *The Pueblo Indians of San Ildefonso.* Columbia U. Press. New York, 1946.

LAGUNA *(läh-goo'-näh)* — *Spanish word for "lake". Native name is* *__Kawaik__* *- meaning unknown.* **Language** - *Keresan.* **Reservation** - *411,833 acres.* **Population** - *4,840; resident - 2,960.* **Government** - *secular officers elected annually by adult male tribal members. Constitution adopted in 1958.* **Dances:** *Sept. 19 - Corn Dance and fiesta. Dec. 24 - Christmas Eve dance.*

Laguna, founded in 1699, is the most recent of New Mexico's pueblos. It was founded by Cochiti and Santo Domingo rebels who had survived De Vargas's attack on their stronghold at La Cieneguilla in 1694. Later they were joined by members of other pueblos; the clans at Laguna trace their origins to Acoma, Zuni, San Felipe, Zia, Oraibi, Sandia, and Jemez.

The population of Laguna, formerly concentrated at the mother village, now also occupies seven nearby settlements: Paguate, Encinal, Paraje, New Laguna, Mesita, Casa Blanca, and Seama. The latter community includes three "suburbs" with the quaint sounding names of Harrisburg, Philadelphia and New York.

Governor Cubero, who visited the pueblo the year it was founded, named it San Jose de la Laguna. A mission was built at the village in 1706 under the direction of Friar Miranda.

The introduction of Presbyterianism at Laguna in 1870 by two Anglos who had married Laguna women resulted in bitter factionalism between conservative elements and the converts of the new religion. A Presbyterian mission was built at the pueblo in 1875, and the new sect succeeded in electing the outsiders to the position of village governor. In protest the conservatives closed their kivas, removed their religious objects, and left the pueblo; most of them migrated to Isleta where they founded the colony of Oraibi. A few took up residence at Mesita. This exodus left Laguna without a religion-oriented leadership.

The tribal government of the Lagunas is perhaps the most progressive of all the pueblos. The sizable income from uranium leases is invested in scholarship programs and local projects which provide employment for the Indians. An electronic plant located on their reservation has proved to be a successful venture for both the owners and the tribe. Most Lagunas take an active part in tribal elections; those who live away from the pueblo make use of absentee ballots.

Most of the Lagunas earn their living at wage work though a small number still do some farming and stock raising.

Because of the heterogeneous make-up of Laguna's population it is not surprising to find that their crafts closely resemble those of other pueblos. Pottery is almost indistinguishable from Acoma ware, plaited yucca baskets are identical to those of the Jemez, and kachina dolls resemble ones made at Zuni. Little craft work is done today, however, except for embroidery.

HARVEY CAPLIN

Sanctuary of the church at Laguna. The Indian influence in the painting at the bottom of the altar is reminiscent of old Zia pottery designs.

MARK BAHTI

Laguna's church dates from 1706.

SUGGESTED READING

Ellis, Florence H. "An Outline of Laguna Pueblo History and Social Organization". *Southwestern Journal of Anthropology.* Vol. 15. No. 4, 1959.

NAMBE

(nähm-bāy') — this is the native name meaning "pueblo of the mound of earth". **Language** - *Tewa.* **Reservation** - *19,115 acres.* **Population** - *285; resident* - *135.* **Government** - *tribal officials elected by members of pueblo.* **Dances:** *Oct. 4 - fiesta.*

To all appearances, there is little to distinguish Nambe from any rural Spanish-American community in the Rio Grande Valley. Only the kiva immediately identifies it as an Indian settlement. The extensive outlines of old walls show that Nambe has declined considerably in size since its founding in the early 1300's.

Intermarriage with the local Spanish-American population has been responsible for a weakening of tribal authority and a gradual breakdown of native life. Despite a recent revival of ceremonialism — typical of a general trend in many Rio Grande pueblos during the past few years — there is little doubt that the native culture will eventually disappear as it has done at Pojoaque.

Because wage work in nearby towns is the most important source of income, less than one half of Nambe's enrolled population lives at the village. Opportunities to earn a living on the reservation are very limited although some income is derived from farming and stock raising.

Nambe Falls, a picturesque recreational area, has been developed by the pueblo and is open to the public; a nominal entrance fee is charged.

MARK BAHTI

Kiva at Nambe Pueblo.

POJOAQUE

(pō-hwä'-key) — Spanish corruption of the native name Posunwage meaning "drink water place". **Language** - *Tewa (formerly).* **Reservation** - *11,592 acres.* **Population** - *85; resident* - *40.* **Government** - *governor chosen by mutual consent of villagers. No dances or ceremonies.*

Pojoaque no longer exists as an Indian community but merely as a reservation. There is nothing in the appearance of this village to distinguish it from any other rural community in northern New Mexico.

The reservation was established in 1946 for the descendents of the original pueblo. This group forms the landholding unit which handles the leasing of its commercial holdings on the highway.

There are no native ceremonies performed at Pojoaque but some of the inhabitants participate in the dances of neighboring Tewa-speaking pueblos.

ZUNI *(zoo'-nee)* — ***Spanish version of the Keresan name Sunyi for this pueblo. The Zuni name for themselves is A'shiwi, meaning "the flesh".*** **Language** - ***Zunian.*** **Reservation** - ***406,967 acres.*** **Population** - ***5,180; resident - 4,200.*** **Government** - ***tribal officers elected biennially by adult members.*** **Dances:** ***late November or early December - Shalako. Kachina dances - spring and summer months. (inquire locally).***

Archaeological evidence indicates that the distinctive culture of the Zunis is the result of a blending of at least two diverse cultural groups in prehistoric times. This "melting pot" situation continued well into historic times as the Zuni continued to absorb into their population Indians from other areas including a number of Tlascalans from central Mexico who had formed a part of Coronado's expedition. Linguistically Zuni is unrelated to any other tribe in the Southwest.

At the beginning of the historic period the Zuni, numbering well over 3,000, occupied six villages in the broad Zuni Valley; the largest of these was Hawikuh. The present pueblo is built on the old site of Halona, one of the original towns which made up the Province of Shiwona.

In 1539 Fray Marcos de Niza set out from Mexico to determine if this settlement could be the fabled Seven Cities of Cibola which reportedly held the treasure of Montezuma. His advance scouting party was led by Estevan, a Moorish slave who had explored the Gulf of Mexico and Texas with Cabeza de Vaca. His earlier successes in dealing with Indian tribes failed him at Zuni. The Indians found his lordly attitude obnoxious and cured his bad manners by killing him shortly after he reached Hawikuh.

After receiving news of Estevan's death De Niza traveled only far enough to get a glimpse of Hawikuh before retracing his steps to Mexico. There, in a report unbecoming a man of the cloth, he announced he had found the Kingdom of Cibola.

The following year Francisco Coronado led an expedition to Zuni. He attacked and captured Hawikuh only to discover that De Niza's glowing report was a hoax.

The Franciscans built a mission at Hawikuh in 1629; the presence of the missionaries caused dissension among the Zuni and resulted in the death of two friars in 1632. The Zunis then fled to a fortified village on Towayalane (Corn Mountain), a precipitous mesa southeast of Zuni.

Outwardly the Zunis appeared to accept Spanish rule, but actually followed a course of passive (and sometimes not so passive) resistance to this new authority.

Raids by Apaches increased in intensity during the late 1600's and finally led to the abandonment of Hawikuh in 1672.

The Zuni supported the Pueblo Rebellion of 1680 but were less involved in it because of their remoteness from the Spanish settlements. Once

Zuni pottery and figurines.

K. C. DEN DOOVEN

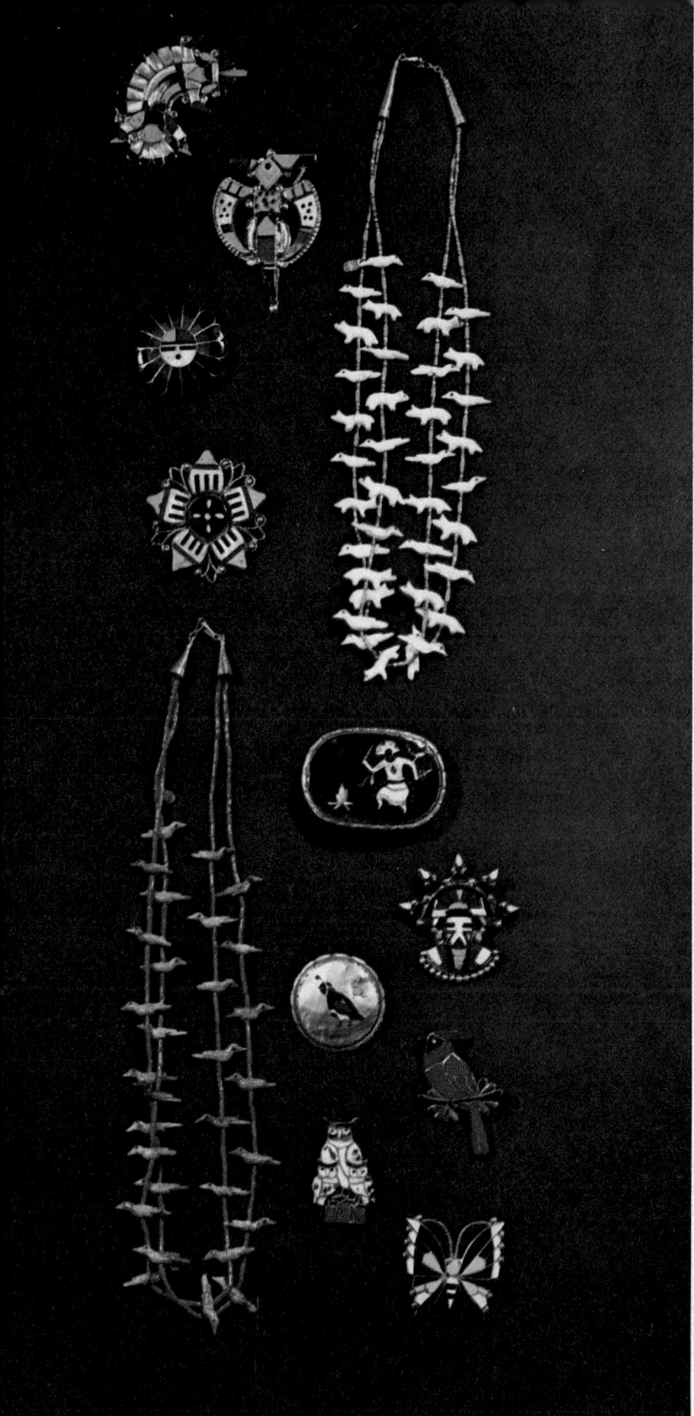
Modern Zuni jewelry.

again they retreated to Corn Mountain and remained there until De Vargas persuaded them to return to the valley in 1692 and resettle at the site of Halona. A new church was built in the village in 1699. (It was abandoned in the early 1800's).

Externally Zuni gives the impression of a very progressive pueblo. It does, however, maintain much of its native life, particularly its religious activities. Perhaps the best known and most spectacular of its many ceremonies is the Shalako, a house blessing ritual which occurs in early December, and includes huge bird-like kachina figures (the couriers of the rain makers) which dance in the Shalako houses.

Subsistence farming and stock raising, supplemented by wage work and seasonal employment such as fire fighting, form the economic base of the village. Jewelry making is also an important source of revenue. An estimated 900 silversmiths and stone cutters (both men and women are skilled in this craft) work part-time at this trade. Pottery production has decreased because it pays less well than jewelry making. Weaving and basketry have almost disappeared.

SUGGESTED READING

Bunzel, Ruth. "Introduction to Zuni Ceremonialism" *Annual Report* No. 47. Bureau of American Ethnology. Washington, D.C. 1932.

Dutton, Bertha P. *Friendly People, The Zuni Indians.* Museum of New Mexico Press. Santa Fe, 1963.

Stevenson, M.C. "The Zuni Indians". *Annual Report* No. 23. Bureau of American Ethnology. Washington, D.C. 1904.

HARVEY CAPLIN

Zuni potter; only a few women continue to practice this ancient craft.

Family activities are carried on in cool brush shelters during the summer months.

JOSEF MUENCH

NAVAJO ***(nă'-väh-hō) from the Tewa word Navahu meaning "cultivated fields". Also spelled Navaho (Navajo has been adopted as the preferred spelling by the tribal government). Native name - DINE' meaning "the people".*** **Language** - ***Athabascan.*** **Reservations** - ***Navajo, Canoncito, Puertocito, and Ramah. Total land area - 15,132,143 acres.*** **Population** - ***over 100,000.*** **Government** - ***constitution adopted - 1938. Tribal council consists of 74 delegates from 18 districts elected by adult members of tribe. Chairman and vice-chairman elected at large.***

The common ancestors of the Navajos and Apaches reached the Southwest shortly after 1000 A.D. as small nomadic bands of hunters and gatherers. Linguistically they were related to the Athabascan-speaking tribes of northwestern Canada. The way of life of each band was modified by its contact with other tribes. The Navajo were particularly influenced by the Pueblo Indians; weaving, agriculture, sandpainting, ceremonial rituals, and matrilineal clans were some of the new traits they acquired. As agriculture grew in economic importance the Navajo became less nomadic and began to settle in small communities near their fields.

A Spanish reference to "Apache de Navajo" as a semi-sedentary agricultural people appears in 1626. It is the first mention of the Navajo which distinguished them from the Apaches. Contact with the Spanish had far-reaching effects on both the Navajo and the Spaniards. With the acquisition of sheep and goats the Indians began to lead a life which was more pastoral than agricultural. The use of the horse allowed them to increase their raiding activities, much to the sorrow of Indian and Spanish communities of the Rio Grande valley. The Navajos considered their forays not as war but rather as an economic pursuit that yielded livestock, food, booty, women, and slaves. (The great use of Indian slaves by the Spanish probably stimulated this activity). For this reason the Navajos were never interested in driving the Spaniards out of the Southwest as the pueblo tribes were.

In 1745 the Franciscans made an attempt to establish missions among the Navajo of the Mount Taylor region. After two years the Indians rejected the new religion but remained friendly to the Spanish. Because of this peaceful coexistence the Navajo of Canyoncito and Puertocito are still known by their fellow tribesmen as "the people who are enemies".

When the Americans assumed jurisdiction of New Mexico in 1846 they sought to control the Navajo by establishing military posts in their country. Without understanding the political makeup of the tribe the U. S. military signed peace treaties with several "chiefs". Actually the "chiefs" were merely headmen whose authority

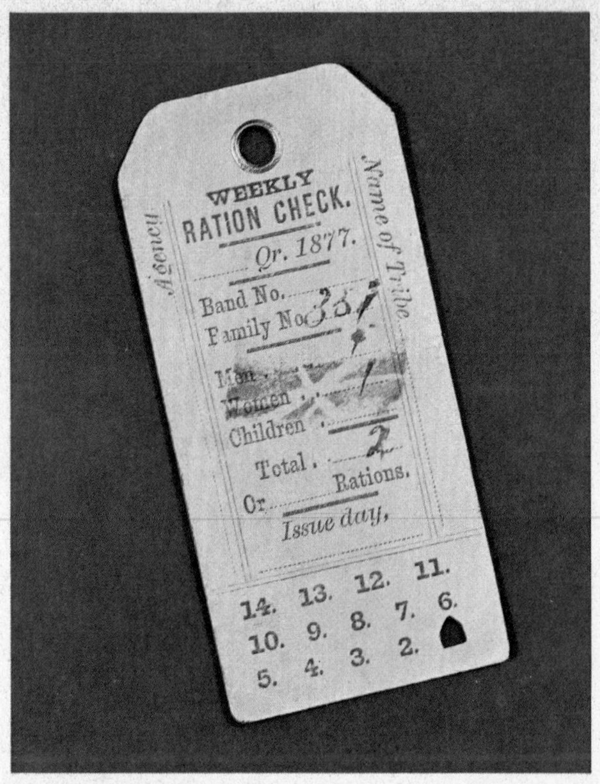

Ration tickets (left) were issued to Navajo families after their release from Bosque Redondo. This one, used only once, was found in a cache in Canyon del Muerto.

Brass and aluminum trade tokens, (bottom) called ***seco peso*** *- "dry money" - because of their light weight, were first used in the 1850's. Their use was officially abolished in 1935 but it still continues in some areas to the present day.*

Fashion-conscious Navajo women concern themselves with the placement of the silver buttons on their blouses in much the same manner that their white sisters worry about the length of their hemlines.

K. C. DEN DOOVEN

did not extend beyond their own small bands. Naturally, raiding by other bands continued since they had not taken part in the negotiations.

By 1863 Navajo depredations became so serious that a military force under Colonel Kit Carson was dispatched to subdue the tribe. Carson accomplished this objective not through military engagements, but by wiping out the economic basis of Navajo life. Livestock was slaughtered and crops, fruit trees, and hogans were completely destroyed.

By March of 1864, 2,400 Navajos had been rounded up to begin the 300 mile journey to their place of confinement at Fort Sumner on the Pecos River in southeastern New Mexico. Eventually some 8,000 men, women and children made "The

WESTERN WAYS

Long Walk" to captivity. An estimated 1,800 avoided capture by hiding out in the more inaccessible areas of their country.

Conditions at the Bosque Redondo reservation were miserable, and more than 2,000 Navajos died from disease before the government decided the relocation plan was a failure. In 1868 the Navajos were allowed to return to their homeland. This move was prompted not so much by humane motives as economy; it would be cheaper to help the Navajo become self-supporting than to keep them in confinement. But their troubles were not over; the white man had not yet lost his taste for Indian land, and clashes occurred over territorial disputes. The schools promised in the treaty of 1868 were run like reformatories and did much to maintain a

Navajo herders in Monument Valley; their country is long on scenery but short on resources.

Fetishes of sheep and goats, carved from shell by the Zunis, are highly prized by the Navajos as effective protection for their flocks and herds.

hostile attitude toward whites.

Despite these problems the Navajos did make a comeback and became self-sufficient. Sheep and cattle were now the basis of Navajo economy; a lively trade was maintained in wool and hides; Navajo rugs and silver work found a ready market. The Navajos prospered and increased in numbers. From an estimated 12,000 in 1868, they grew to 35,000 in 1930.

By the 1930's the basis of Navajo life—sheep—had increased to the point where the land was seriously overgrazed and erosion became a major problem. Only one solution was possible—drastic stock reduction—another critical blow to Navajo life.

Despite its size (roughly the area of West Virginia) the reservation has limited resources and much of the land is absolutely worthless except as scenery. Thousands of Navajos leave the reservation to seek employment; many find seasonal jobs as migrant agricultural workers. Craft work, while it provides income for individuals, is of minor importance in the over-all economy.

Considerable tribal income is derived from gas and oil leases and timber sales. Much of this income is being invested in tribal enterprises which will provide jobs for Indians on the reservation.

Serious problems still face the tribe but for the Navajos adversity has long been a constant condition.

SUGGESTED READING

Dyk, Walter (recorder). *Son of Old Man Hat, A Navajo Autobiography*. Harcourt, Brace 1938.

Kluckhohn, Clyde and Dorothea C. Leighton. *The Navajo*. Harvard U. Press, Cambridge, 1946.

Link, Martin A., *Navajo: A Century of Progress, 1868-1968)*. Navajo Tribe, Window Rock, 1968.

Underhill, Ruth. *Here Come the Navaho!* U.S. Indian Service: Indian Life and Customs, No. 8. Lawrence, Kansas, 1953.

PHOTOGRAPHS BY K. C. DEN DOOVEN

Old Navajo pawn jewelry.

UTAH
NAVAJO
ARIZONA
PAIUTE
NEVADA
Colorado River
NAVAJO AND HOPI
HOPI
HAVASUPAI
HUALAPAI
NAVAJO
FLAGSTAFF
MOHAVE
HUALAPAI
YAVAPAI
CHEMEHUEVI
Bill Williams River
MOHAVE
CALIFORNIA
COLORADO RIVER RESERVATION
Colorado River
WHITE MOUNTAIN APACHE
YAVAPAI
Salt River
SAN CARLOS APACHE
CHEMEHUEVI
PHOENIX
PIMA AND MARICOPA
River
YUMA
PAPAGO
PIMA
Gila
COCOPA
TUCSON
PAPAGO
PAPAGO
PAPAGO
PAPAGO

SAN JUAN

WESTERN APACHE

ZUNI

JICARILLA APACHE

JICARILLA APACHE

INDIAN RESERVATIONS OF THE SOUTHWEST

HOPI *(hoe'-pee) the name is a contraction of* *Hopi-tuh* *their tribal name which means "the peaceful ones".* **Language** - *Shoshonean.* **Reservation** - *631,194 acres.* **Population** - *5,200.* **Government** - *constitution adopted 1936. Hopi tribal council made up of seventeen members elected by villages according to population. Chairman and vice-chairman selected by council. Not all villages recognize the authority of the Hopi tribal council and continue to follow their traditional form of village government which recognizes the* *Kikmongwi* *(village priest-chief) as the authority. Much factionalism has resulted from the insistence of the U.S. government that the Hopi be dealt with as a single tribe rather than as separate pueblos in the manner of the Rio Grande villages.* **Ceremonials** - *Kachina dances are performed from January until late July. Unmasked dances, including the well-known Snake Dance, begin in August and continue through December.*

Hopi tradition tells of the people inhabiting three underworlds before emerging into the present one. The settlement of land is explained in terms of individual clans which wandered about and occupied many sites prior to settling in their present villages. There is no doubt that the Hopi tribe is made up of numerous groups of diverse origins.

The people of Walpi built their village on this narrow mesa top as a defense against the Spaniards. RAY MANLEY

At first appearance the arid mesa country of the Hopi appears incapable of supporting a permanent population. Yet this agricultural tribe has not only existed but thrived in a hostile environment. Tiny springs at the mesa edge, fed by the drainage of Black Mesa, have sustained the Hopis for many hundreds of years. Because of their expertness at dry farming they have been able to grow their crops of corn, squash, beans, and cotton on land that would give nightmares to Midwestern farmers.

A short (133 days) growing season and limited (12 inches per year) rainfall made it imperative to obtain the help of supernatural forces to insure adequate moisture and bountiful harvests. It was only natural that this would be the focus of Hopi religious activities. Much time was spent in performing complex and beautiful rituals and dances to bring about the desired results. Today the Hopi still maintain one of the most elaborate religious calendars of all Southwestern tribes.

At the time of Spanish contact in 1540 the

Hopi occupied seven politically independent villages. The Hopi submitted to Spanish rule after Pedro de Tovar attacked and defeated the pueblo of Kawaikuh. Onate, in 1598, received formal promises of loyalty from the Hopi but because they remained on the Spanish frontier no civil authority was established among them nor were they required to pay tribute to the Crown. The Hopi were subjected to missionary activities in the 1600's when the Franciscans established missions in several of the villages but Spanish influence was much less intensive than among the Rio Grande pueblos. New crops, fruit trees, livestock, and metal tools were acquired but religious and political life were virtually untouched. The Spanish system of selecting governors for secular offices was never adopted.

Nevertheless the Hopi were anxious to rid themselves of any Spanish control and joined the eastern pueblos in the revolt of 1680. Resident priests were killed and the missions destroyed and the Hopi remained hostile to all subsequent attempts to re-establish Spanish authority. Only one village, Awatobi, remained friendly and it was attacked and destroyed by the other Hopi pueblos and the survivors absorbed into the villages of the attackers.

Hopis maintained friendly relations with most tribes and traveled great distances to trade with other people. (Hopi weaving is still much sought after by the Rio Grande pueblos). Occasionally in times of drouth, they left their villages to take up temporary residence with the Havasupai and Zuni. The Navajo, who harassed the Hopi with their constant raiding, were regarded as traditional enemies.

Anglo contact, which began in 1826, has had a much greater effect on Hopi life. Policies of the Bureau of Indian Affairs and the influence of Christian missionaries have resulted in considerable factionalism among the Hopi villages and disruption of their way of life. Nevertheless it is apparent that the Hopi have retained much of their native culture.

Farming and stock raising are still important economic pursuits among the Hopi although wage work provides the bulk of individual income. No tribe produces a greater quantity or variety of craft work than the Hopi; basketry, pottery, kachina dolls, silverwork, and weaving of excellent quality find a ready market both on and off the reservation.

Unlike the Rio Grande pueblos, Hopi dances —both masked (kachina) and unmasked — are open to the general public. The dances, certainly as beautiful and impressive as any in the world, are dramatized prayers for rain, the growth of

Hopi pottery from First Mesa.

PHOTOGRAPHS BY K. C. DEN DOOVEN

Three kachinas which play the part of clowns.

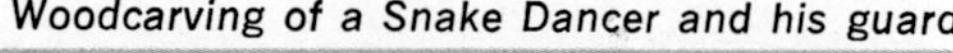

Woodcarving of a Snake Dancer and his guard.

Ceremonial garments; men are the weavers among the Hopi.

crops, and for the health and well-being of not only the Hopi but all people.

First Mesa

WALPI — (wal'-pee) — "place of the gap." The people of Walpi occupied two earlier sites on the lower terrace of First Mesa before moving to their present location in 1680. Fear of a Spanish reprisal for their part in the Pueblo Rebellion prompted the change to a more defensive position. The move worked well, for neither of two punitive expeditions sent by the Spaniards attacked the village because of its impregnable appearance. Snake Dance is performed during odd numbered years. *Polacca,* the community at the foot of the mesa, was settled in the late 1800's by First Mesa people who wished to live near the trading post and day school.

SICHOMOVI — (si-cho'-mo-vee) "place of the mound where wild currants grow" was founded about 1750 as a colony of Walpi.

HANO — (ha'-no) — the Hopi name for this Tewa village may be derived from "anopi" which means "eastern people" or a corruption of Los Tanos, the Spanish name for the Tewas. A popular story claims Hano is a nickname because of the frequent use of "ha" in Tewa speech. Hano was settled by Tewa refugees from the Rio Grande valley after the Pueblo Rebellion. The Hopi claim the Tewa sought refuge from the Spanish; the Tewa claim the Hopi asked them to help protect Walpi. The argument is as old as the village. Despite their long association with the Hopi the Tewa people retain their own language and religious customs. Nampeyo, the potter who was responsible for the revival of Hopi pottery in 1890, was a Tewa from Hano.

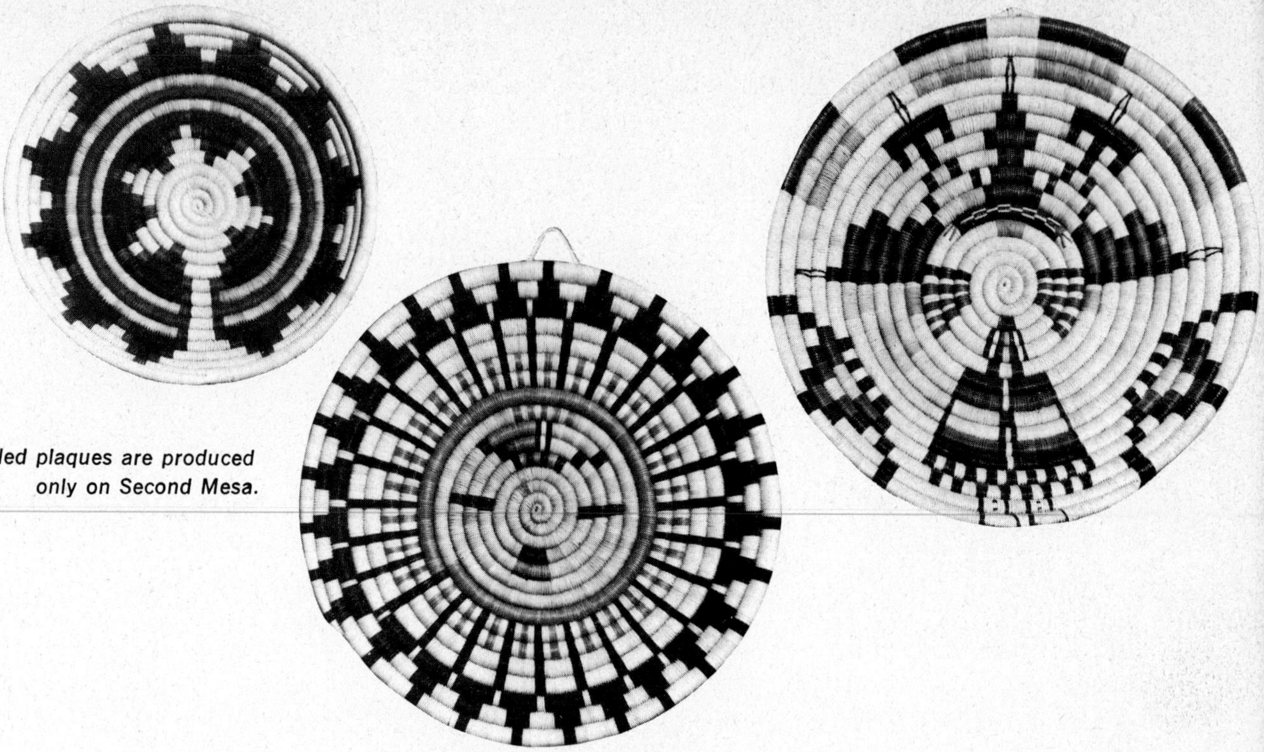

Coiled plaques are produced only on Second Mesa.

Shipaulovi. The whiteman's electric light poles fail to blend with the landscape the way Hopi architecture does.

K. C. DEN DOOVEN

Aerial view of Hotevilla village; walled gardens are clustered near the spring at the foot of the mesa. Scattered peach trees dot the mesa top.

Second Mesa

SHUNGOPOVI — (shung-o'-po-vee) "place by the spring where the tall reeds grow" is the most important of the villages on Second Mesa. Two earlier pueblos were located in the foothills below the mesa near Gray Spring. The Franciscan mission of San Bartolome was built at Old Shungopovi in 1629. It was destroyed during the Revolt of 1680 and the village abandoned in favor of the present mesa-top location. Snake Dance is performed during even-numbered years.

MISHONGNOVI—(mi-shong'-no-vee) "place of the black man" derives its name from Mishong, leader of the Crow Clan who brought his people to Hopi from the San Francisco Peaks region in 1200 A.D. The people of Shungopovi allowed them to settle at Corn Rock, a Shungopovi shrine, with the understanding that they would protect it against the First Mesa people. In 1629 the Franciscans built the chapel of San Buenaventura at Mishongnovi. It was destroyed and the village abandoned in 1680. The present pueblo was established shortly thereafter. Snake Dance is performed during odd-numbered years.

SHIPAULOVI — (shi-paw'-lo-vee) "the mosquitoes" was, according to tradition, settled by people from Homolobi, a prehistoric pueblo on the Little Colorado River (near the present town of Winslow) which was abandoned because of the swarms of mosquitoes which infested the area. A more likely explanation is that Shipaulovi was established after the Pueblo Revolt by people from Shungopovi so that in the event that the Spaniards should return and destroy their village Shipaulovi would be able to carry on its ceremonies and religious traditions.

Third Mesa

ORAIBI — (o-rye'-bee) "place of the rock called Orai" claims (along with Acoma) to be the oldest continuously inhabited town in the United States. It dates from about 1150 A.D. According to tradition Oraibi was founded by a dissident group from Old Shungopovi. In 1629 the mission of San Francisco was established at Oraibi; the ruins of this church are north of the village. (An abandoned Mennonite church stands on the mesa edge). Oraibi, with a population of 1,200, was the largest Hopi village until 1906 when a split occurred over ceremonial prerogatives and Bureau of Indian Affairs policies. The problem was settled bloodlessly with a "push of war". The losers, led

Moenkopi village and irrigated fields.

The "push of war", which settled the difference between rival factions at Oraibi, was commemorated by this inscription in 1906.

by Yukioma, left Oraibi and built a new village, Hotevilla. An inscription which commemorates the Oraibi split is carved in the bedrock north of the village; it reads "Well, it have to be this way now, that when you pass me over this line it will be done, Sept. 8, 1906". The clan symbols of the two opposing leaders are also included.

KIAKOCHOMOVI — (kee-ah-ko'-chom-o-vee) "place of the hills of ruins" also called Lower Oraibi or New Oraibi was settled in 1890 by Oraibi people who wanted to live near the school and trading post.

HOTEVILLA—(hote'-vil-la) "skinned back". The name is derived from the village spring which is located in a cave with a low overhang. The village was settled in 1906 by the conservative faction from Oraibi. Hotevilla has a long history of non-cooperation with the federal government and is still regarded as the most conservative Hopi village.

BAKABI — (bah'-ka-bee) "place of the jointed reeds" was settled in 1907 by a group which left the newly-founded village of Hotevilla and attempted to return to Oraibi. They were refused admittance so they established their own village rather than return to Hotevilla.

MOENKOPI — (mu'-en'ko'pee) "place of running water" is the westernmost of the Hopi villages. It was originally a farming settlement of Oraibi but was established as a separate village in the 1870's by Tuvi, an Oraibi leader. Because its traditions are related to Oraibi, it is included here as a Third Mesa village although it is located forty miles to the west. Moenkopi is the only Hopi village with irrigated fields.

SUGGESTED READING

Dozier, Edward P. *Hano, Tewa Indian Community In Arizona.* Holt Rinehart and Winston. New York, 1966.

Nequatewa, Edmund. *Truth of a Hopi.* Museum of Northern Arizona. Flagstaff, 1967.

Talayesva, Don. *Sun Chief: The Autobiography of a Hopi Indian.* Ed. by L. W. Simmons. Yale University Press. New Haven, 1942.

Thompson, Laura. *Culture in Crisis: A Study of the Hopi Indians.* Harper, New York, 1950.

Thompson, Laura and Alice Joseph. *The Hopi Way.* U. of Chicago Press. Chicago, 1950.

Modern Hopi jewelry; overlay silverwork was begun in 1935 at the encouragement of the Museum of Northern Arizona. Sandcast and inlaid pieces are the work of Charles Loloma.

PAIUTE *(pie'-yoōt or päh'-yoōt)* ***The origin of the name is uncertain although "true Ute" has been suggested as translation of the native name.*** **Language** - ***Shoshonean.*** **Reservation** - ***(Arizona only) - Kaibab 121,000 acres.*** **Population** - ***135.*** **Government** - ***Kaibab reservation - constitution adopted - 1951. Members elect tribal council of six persons. Council selects tribal officers. Other bands of Paiutes occupy reservations in Nevada and Utah.***

The Kaibab band, a branch of the Southern Paiute, originally ranged over portions of northwestern Arizona, southern Utah, and southeastern Nevada.

The Paiute economy was based on food gathering. They led a semi-nomadic existence in order to make maximum use of whatever wild foods were available. Their extensive use of edible roots earned them the name of "Diggers" from contemptuous whites but even the most ethnocentric Anglo had to admit that the Paiutes could exist in a land where a whiteman would quickly starve to death. Nothing was overlooked as food: pine nuts, wild grass seeds—even grasshoppers and caterpillars. Big game was scarce so the Indians caught rabbits, birds, gophers, prairie dogs, and mice.

Life for the Paiute was a constant search for food and it left little time to develop elaborate crafts, social or religious organizations. The land would not support large concentrations of people so most groups consisted of two or three families. Leaders had no formal authority over their followers. There were no tribal ceremonies except for social dances. Medicine men conducted simple curing and hunting rituals.

The Kaibab Paiute had some contact with Utes and learned from them the use of buckskin clothing, the horse, and the tipi which replaced their earlier earth covered lodges.

Buckskin and basketry were the two main crafts of the Kaibab band. Burden baskets, trays for parching wild seeds, and hats were made using a twining technique. Coiled baskets in bowl and bottle shapes were made of sumac. The Navajo "wedding basket" usually attributed to the Paiutes and Utes was never made by this band. (A group of Southern Utes who moved into the San Juan River area—and called Pah (water) Utes—made these baskets and traded them to the Navajo).

The Kaibab reservation was established in 1917. The land is suitable only for cattle raising although some garden plots are farmed. Income from a tribal herd and wage work make up the economy of these people.

SUGGESTED READING

Kelly, Isabel T. "Southern Paiute Ethnography". *Utah U. Anthropological Papers No. 69.* Salt Lake City, 1964.

CHEMEHUEVI *(tchĕm-ĕ-hwāy'-vee)* ***— the Yuman name for the Paiutes of southeastern California - meaning unknown. Native name is <u>Nüwü</u> meaning "The People".*** **Language** - ***Shoshonean.*** **Reservation** - ***Colorado River (shared with several other tribes) 265,850 acres, 225,995 acres of which are in Arizona.*** **Population** ***- 680.*** **Government** - ***constitution adopted in 1937. Tribal officers selected by nine member council. Council members elected biennially for four-year terms.***

The use of present day political boundaries to identify and locate Indian tribes in prehistoric times does more to confuse than enlighten. State lines are accepted as logical dividing lines for closely related tribes, and little regard is shown for the natural geographical boundaries which cross the neat but imaginary lines drawn on maps.

Thus it is that the Chemehuevi are usually listed as a "California desert tribe" when in reality they are linguistically and culturally part of the Great Basin culture which occupied the major portion of what is now Nevada and Utah.

A small tribe of about 800, they led a semi-

Chemehuevi baskets

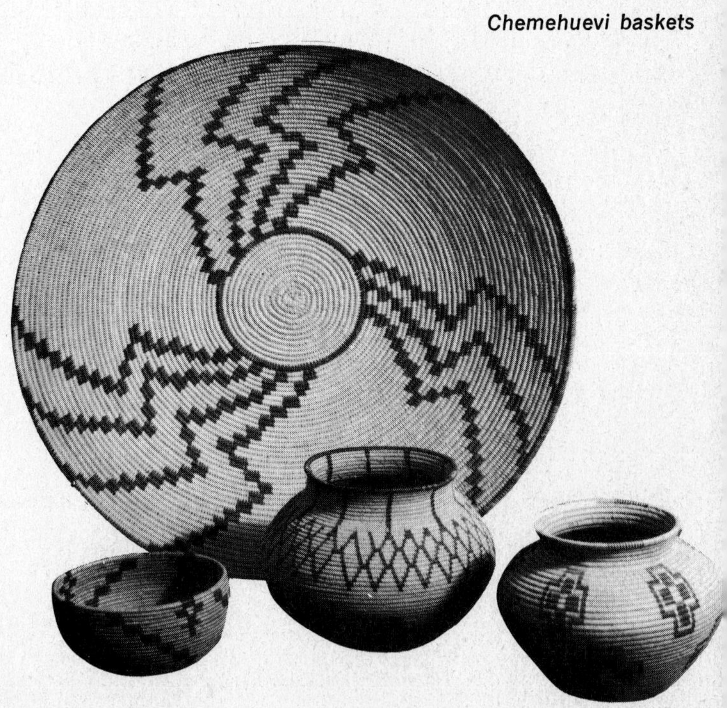

K. C DEN DOOVEN

Trays for winnowing wild grass seeds and baskets for gathering edible insects were used by the Paiutes in eking out a living in an unfriendly land.

nomadic life in the eastern half of the Mojave Desert. Extensive use of wild plants supplemented by small game allowed the Chemehuevis to eke out an existence in this inhospitable region. Small bands, sometimes no more than an extended family unit, ranged over wide areas to gather sufficient quantities of seeds, roots, and berries. It was much more practical to move a camp to the food supply than to maintain permanent settlements. The necessity to roam constantly did not permit the development of strong tribal unity, complex social organization, or elaborate rituals and ceremonies.

In the late 1700's the Chemehuevis moved into Mohave territory on the west side of the Colorado River. This contact resulted in the acquisition of a number of Yuman traits including mourning ceremonies, power derived from dreams, and Mohave mythology.

In 1867 hostilities disrupted their friendly relations with the Mohave, and the Chemehuevi withdrew to the desert country to the west. Later, however, they drifted back to occupy the Chemehuevi valley.

A reservation was set aside for this tribe on the California side of the Colorado River, but the construction of Parker Dam in 1938 caused much of the land to be flooded. Most of the Chemehuevis then moved to the Colorado River reservation where they now live. The raising of such cash crops as alfalfa and cotton is the chief occupation of this tribe.

Once noted for their fine coiled baskets of willow and devil's claw, the Chemehuevi no longer practice this craft. Native ceremonies and rituals have also disappeared.

SUGGESTED READING

Kroeber, A. L. *Handbook of the Indians of California.* pp 593-600. California Book Co. 1953.

Hundreds of tribesmen attend the four-day maidens' puberty rite, the most important ceremony of the Apaches.

APACHE ***(äh-păh'-chee) from the Zuni name Apachu for these people meaning "enemy". Native name varies with each tribe but is usually a variation of "Inde, Tinde or Tinneh" all meaning "the people". Language - Athabascan - related linguistically to Athabascan tribes in Canada. (for population and reservations see separate listings).***

Sometime after 1000 A.D. the ancestors of the Apaches entered the Southwest. Following the migrations of buffalo herds these small bands of hunters drifted down from the north. At the time of Spanish contact the division of the original stock into separate tribes was still taking place. The name Apache was applied to all of these people and is still used today as a general term for the individual tribes.

Although contact with other tribes modified the culture of each group they all remained dependent upon hunting and gathering for subsistence. What could not be obtained by these pursuits was stolen from the villages of agricultural tribes.

With the acquisition of horses the range and frequency of their depredations increased until the raiding of Indian, Spanish, and later Mexican and American settlements became a way of life. The Apaches ranged over an area which extended from southern Colorado to northern Mexico and from central Arizona to western Texas.

Numerous unsuccessful attempts were made by the Spaniards, Mexicans, and Americans to exterminate the Apaches. Military campaigns were launched against them, bounties were paid for scalps, captives were kept as slaves, and treacheries of the worst kind were perpetrated in ruthless efforts to put an end to the Apache raiders. But the Apaches refused to die or surrender; what they lacked in numbers they made up in ferocity and cunning. As guerrilla fighters the Apaches were unparalleled. (Because Indians do not write history books the atrocities committed by them are naturally better known than those committed by their enemies).

After the Civil War attempts were made to confine the tribes to reservations so that the settlement of the Southwest by Anglos could proceed. Problems continued as corrupt officials cheated the Indians out of promised rations and turned over large areas of Indian land to whites for mining and agricultural developments. Distrust and discontent resulted and new uprisings occurred.

The last outbreak was led by Geronimo; his small band of Chiricahua renegades terrorized Arizona, New Mexico, and northern Mexico from 1884 until its capture in 1886. This ended the Apache wars but stupidity marched on. The renegades were sent to Florida as prisoners of war *in addition to all Chiricahuas—men, women and children—who had remained peacefully on the reservation and the Apache scouts who had aided the U.S. Army in capturing Geronimo!*

It was not until 1914, after twenty-eight years in military prisons in Florida, Alabama, and Oklahoma that the Chiricahuas were finally released from their prisoner of war status and permitted to return home.

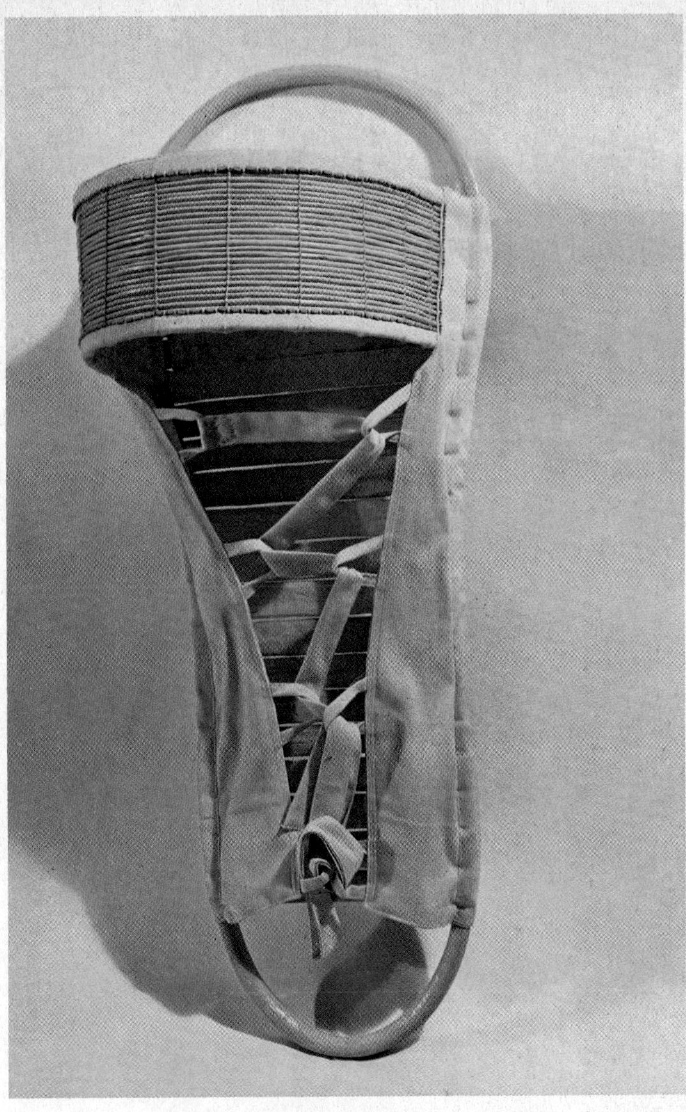

Apache cradleboard. Contrary to a popular myth there is no single "Indian word" which is used for a cradleboard.

The Apache single string violin is made from the hollowed out stalk of the Century plant.

Western Apache

The Athabascan group known as the Western Apache originally consisted of a number of independent subtribes. The present San Carlos and White Mountain "tribes" are comprised of members of these early bands; the Mogollon, Pinaleno, Tonto, Arivaipa, Coyotero and Chiricahua are represented in the San Carlos division. The White Mountain "tribe" is made up of members of the Mimbreno, Mogollon, Pinaleno, Chiricahua and Arivaipa bands.

SAN CARLOS - **Language** - ***Athabascan.*** **Reservation** - ***1,623,444*** **acres. Population** - ***4,000.*** **Government** - ***constitution adopted 1936. Tribal corporate charter - 1940. Tribal council consists of seven elected members.***

WHITE MOUNTAIN - **Language** - ***Athabascan.*** **Reservation** - ***1,684,872*** ***acres.*** **Population** - ***3,850.*** **Government** - ***constitution adopted 1938. Ten member council elected by adult members of the tribe.***

The nomadic bands of hunters which were to be later known as the Western Apaches entered what is now southwestern New Mexico, Arizona, and northern Mexico during the 1500's.

By the latter part of the 16th Century they began to raid Spanish settlements in northern Sonora and Chihuahua. Early Spanish accounts do not refer to these people as Apaches but it is possible that the raiders whom they called Sumas, Jocomes and Janos were either these Athabascan-speaking bands or were later absorbed by them (probably the Chiricahua and Mimbreno Apaches). After 1700 they are referred to merely as Apaches.

Attempts to missionize these people ended in a full-scale rebellion in 1684. To protect their settlements from renewed Apache attacks the Spanish established a line of presidios across northern Mexico but defensive warfare proved useless against the hit-and-run tactics of the Apaches. Besides, the Indians were not interested in driving out the Spaniards but merely in raiding them for horses, cattle and booty. Expeditions against the Apaches in their own territory were equally unsuccessful since pitched battles were avoided by the Indians whenever possible.

The Spaniards then tried a new tactic. Apache bands were encouraged to settle near the presidios where they would receive rations — and liquor — until they became dependent upon the Spanish. The plan worked to a great extent until 1811 when the Mexican government was forced to discontinue the policy for lack of funds and the Manso (tame) Apaches quickly returned to raiding.

Warfare became more intense and widespread as bands pillaged as far south as Hermo-

TAD NICHOLS

Apache Mountain Spirit dancers perform on the last night of the girls' puberty rite.

Typical White Mountain Apache settlemen

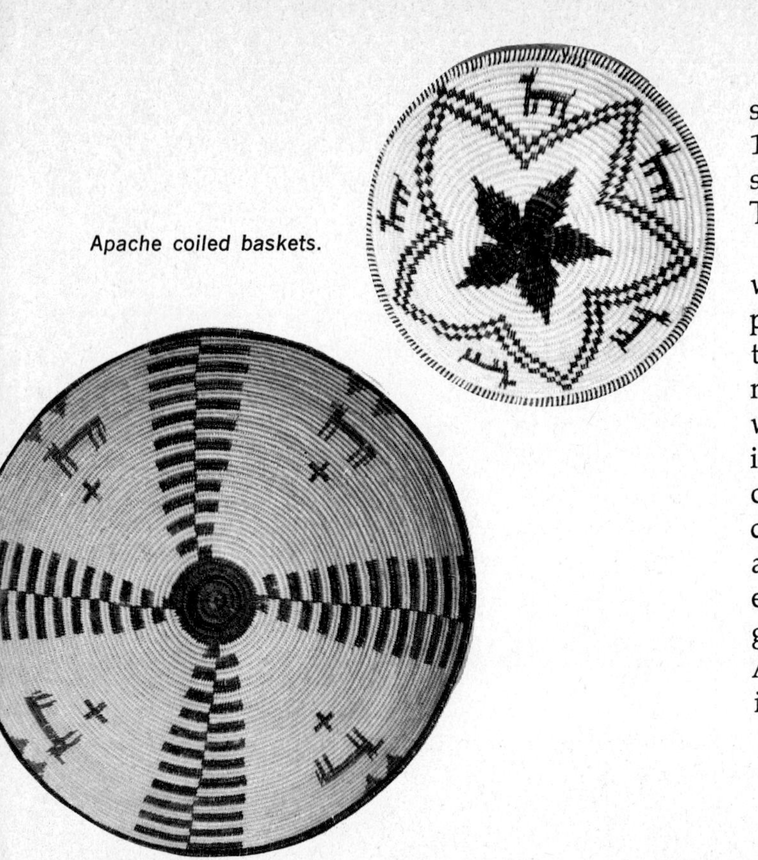

Apache coiled baskets.

sillo, Sonora and west into Papago country. In 1848 Tubac was abandoned along with many other settlements and the Mexicans were pushed south. The Apaches were in control.

Conflicts with Anglos began in the 1820's when beaver trappers, bounty hunters, and prospectors began to invade the Apache domain. Nevertheless, many of the tribes seemed interested in maintaining peaceful relations with the Americans when the U.S. assumed control of Apache country in 1853. Exactly how the Americans could lay claim to Apache territory simply because they had defeated the Mexicans mystified the Apaches; after all, neither the Spaniards nor the Mexicans had ever succeeded in defeating the Apaches! The greatest problem, however, resulted from the Americans' insistence that the Indians cease raiding the Mexican settlements across the border.

TAD NICHOLS

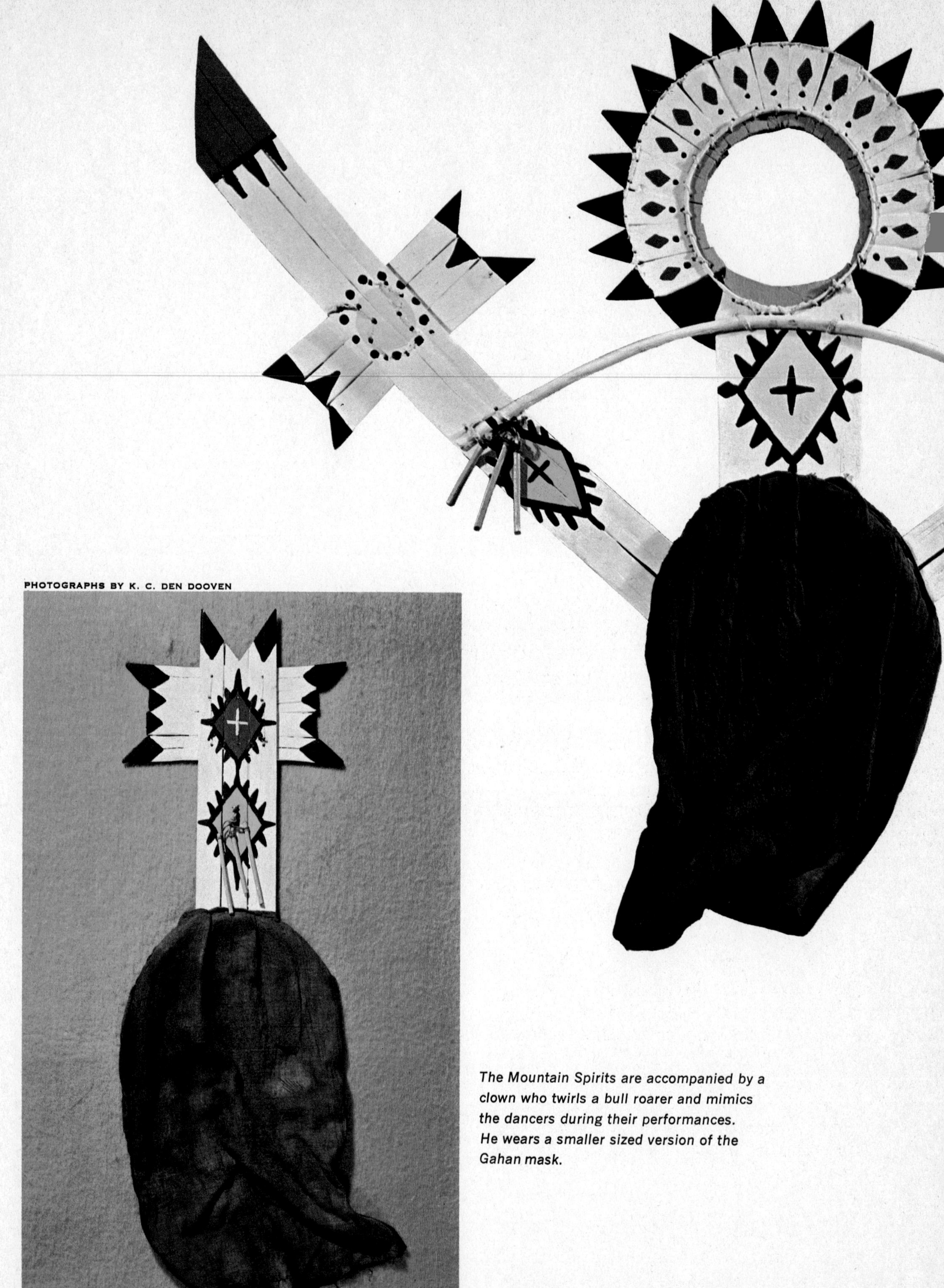

PHOTOGRAPHS BY K. C. DEN DOOVEN

The Mountain Spirits are accompanied by a clown who twirls a bull roarer and mimics the dancers during their performances. He wears a smaller sized version of the Gahan mask.

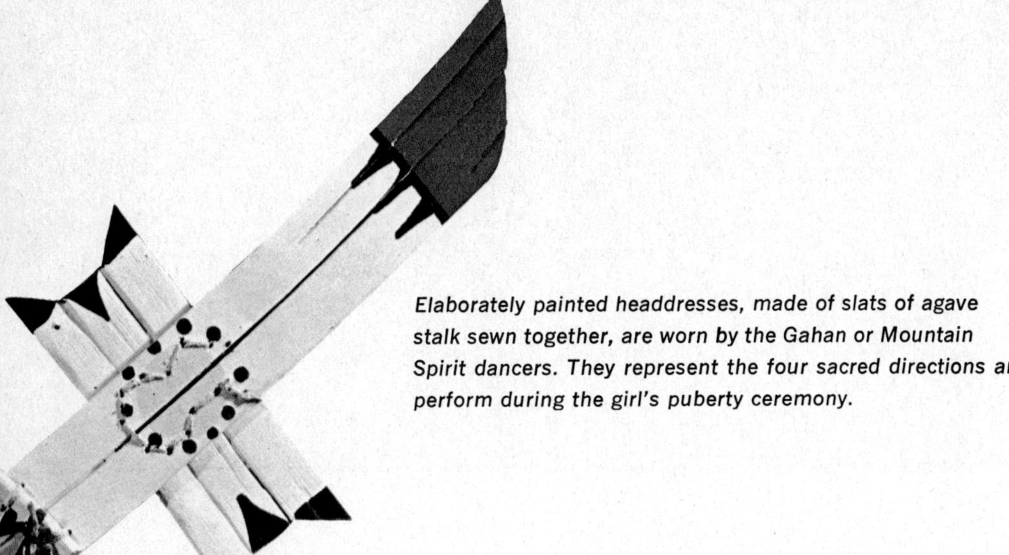

Elaborately painted headdresses, made of slats of agave stalk sewn together, are worn by the Gahan or Mountain Spirit dancers. They represent the four sacred directions and perform during the girl's puberty ceremony.

Attempts to confine the Apaches to reservations were largely unsuccessful because of the prevailing atmosphere of mutual distrust and the period between 1853 and 1889 was marked by constant unrest. Disagreements between civil and military authorities on how best to handle the Indians prevented the formulation of a consistent and constructive policy. White settlers and miners appropriated Apache lands with the help of corrupt administrators. Dissident Apache bands frequently left their reservations to pillage Mexican and American settlements.

It was not until 1890, after seventy bloody years, that the Apaches abandoned their old way of life for more peaceful pursuits.

Today the Western Apaches are among the most progressive tribes in the Southwest. Successful tribal enterprises include stock raising, stores, service stations, a lumber mill and tourist facilities. Individual incomes are derived from farming, wage work, and cattle raising.

Beadwork, cradleboards and some basketry are still being produced though few of these items (except the cradleboards) are being used by the Indians themselves.

SUGGESTED READING

Baldwin, Gordon. *The Warrior Apaches.* Dale King, Publisher, Tucson, 1965.

Opler, Morris E. *An Apache's Life-way.* Cooper Square Publishers. New York, 1965.

Thrapp, Dan L. *The Conquest of Apacheria.* U. of Oklahoma Press. Norman, 1967.

Apache burden basket.

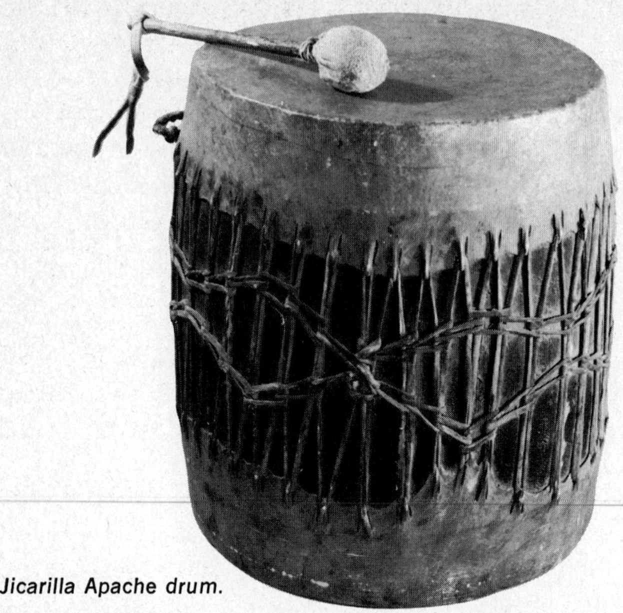

Jicarilla Apache drum.

JICARILLA ***(hē-käh-ree'-ya) The Spanish name for this Apache tribe meaning "small basket" — derived from their production and use of that item. Native name is Tinde meaning "the people". Language - Athabascan Reservation - 722,300 acres. Population - 1,950. Government - constitution adopted in 1937. Tribe operates as a federal corporation. Tribal council, chairman and vice chairman elected by adult tribal members. Ceremonials: Sept. 14-15, Bear Dance and ceremonial race (inquire locally for location).***

At the time of Spanish contact the Jicarillas occupied the mountainous region in the vicinity of Taos and Picuris. Their range extended across northern New Mexico and southern Colorado. Earlier they had roamed the buffalo plains to the southeast but were driven out, along with the Mescaleros, by the Comanches.

From their contact with Pueblo tribes the Jicarillas learned to supplement their hunting economy with some agriculture. They maintained friendly relations with Picuris and Taos but did not hesitate to raid the pueblos between peaceful trading visits. Spanish settlements, however, became the primary targets for they provided the Apaches with a source of horses and livestock. From the Utes, with whom they allied themselves against the Navajo, they acquired a number of Plains Indian traits including buckskin clothing, beadwork, and tipis.

In 1773 the Spaniards established a mission near Taos in an effort to missionize the Jicarillas. It was soon abandoned when the Indians refused to accept a sedentary life under Spanish rule.

The U.S. government in 1853 attempted to settle several hundred Jicarillas on a reservation on the Rio Puerco. It was unsuccessful and the Indians continued their forays against the Americans. Between 1853 and 1887 the Jicarillas were moved no less than eight times before the government made up its mind where the tribe should be settled.

Little remains of the native culture except language and social organization. The only remaining ceremony is the Bear Dance, (borrowed from the Utes) a girls' puberty ritual. A recent attempt has been made to revive the old crafts; buckskin, beadwork, and a limited number of coiled baskets are now being produced.

Economically the Jicarillas are more fortunate than most Southwestern tribes. Considerable income is derived from oil and gas leases and the sale of timber. This income is being invested in tribal enterprises—and education—which will provide jobs for tribal members.

Cattle raising and wage work are important sources of individual income. The Jicarillas also raise sheep but because this activity lacks prestige Navajos are usually hired to do the work.

The reservation, located in high, cool pine country, attracts many visitors who come to hunt, fish, and camp.

SUGGESTED READING

Opler, Morris K. "Summary of Jicarilla Apache Culture". *American Anthropologist*, Vol. 38. 1936.

MESCALERO ***(mess-käh-lair'-ō) — Spanish name for this tribe because of their extensive use of the mescal cactus as a food. Language - Athabascan. Reservation - 460,000 acres. Population - 1,470; resident - 1,245. Government - tribal constitution and bylaws adopted 1936. Tribe operates under federal charter as a corporation. Business committee of ten, which functions as a tribal council, elected biennially by tribal members. Ceremonials: July 1-4 - rodeo and fiesta, includes Gahan (Mt. Spirit) dancers.***

At the time the Spaniards entered the Southwest the main band of the Mescalero tribe occupied the Sierra Blanca Mountains just north of their present reservation. Other bands inhabited the Big Bend country of Texas and the Guadalupe Mountains on the New Mexico-Texas border.

During the summers they lived in the mountains, moving from one campsite to another in search of game and wild plants. Occasionally they made buffalo hunting trips—using dogs as pack animals before the advent of the horse—onto the plains to the east. During these journeys they frequently fought the Comanches who claimed this territory as their own.

In winter they moved into the warmer desert regions where they made great use of desert plants, particularly the mescal cactus. In between they found time to raid the villages of the pueblo Indians in the Rio Grande valley.

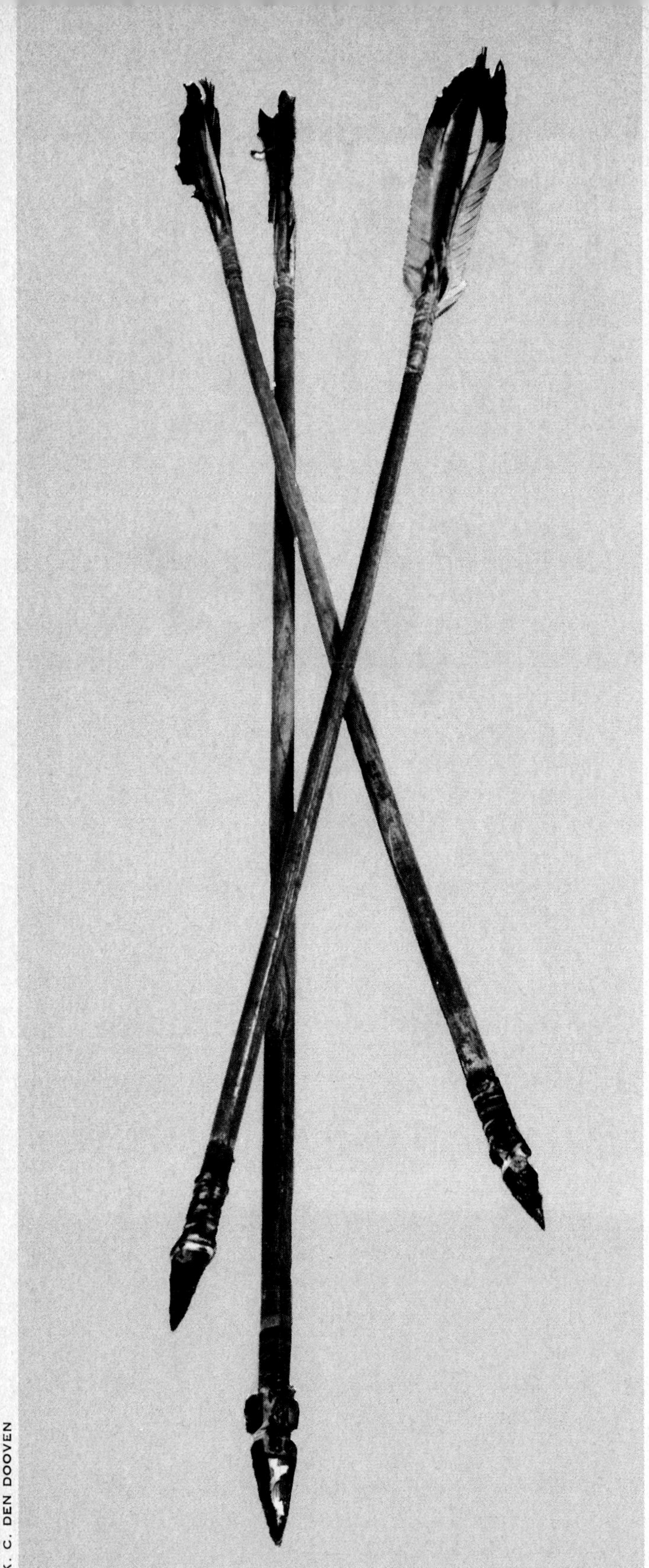

Old Apache arrows.

Their first contacts with the Spanish explorers were friendly but the occupation of their land by colonizers soon changed this. By the late 1680's the Mescaleros presented a serious threat to the Spanish settlements.

In 1788-89 the Spanish launched a military campaign to subdue both the Mescalero and Lipan Apaches. Several defeats and the promise of free rations greatly reduced Apache depredations. Relative peace prevailed until 1811 when the new Mexican government assumed control of the area. Financial troubles prevented continuance of the ration system and the Apaches soon left the settlements to resume raiding as a livelihood.

Attempts to confine the Apache were made by the U.S. in the 1850's. Treaties providing "perpetual peace" and rations were made with the Mescalero but never officially ratified. Raiding, quite naturally, followed and forts were established in the lower Rio Grande valley to protect the white settlers.

After a successful military campaign by U.S. troops in 1855 the Mescalero sued for peace and signed a treaty agreeing to settle at Fort Stanton. The experiment was short-lived as peaceful Mescaleros found themselves the victims of raids by revenge-seeking Mexicans.

General Carleton finally subdued the Mescaleros in 1862. In 1864 about four hundred were confined to Bosque Redondo near Fort Sumner, New Mexico. The remainder escaped to Mexico or went to live with the Western Apache.

Those who remained at Bosque Redondo suffered greatly. Drouth killed their crops; bad water, disease, and Navajo raids decimated their numbers. In 1864 several thousand Navajos rounded up by Kit Carson were also confined on the 40 square mile area with the Mescalero.

Once again the Mescalero drifted back to their land and old way of life.

A reservation was finally established near their home territory in the early 1870's (modified later, of course, to meet the demands of encroaching whites). Programs to "civilize" the Mescalero required them to cut their hair (then, as now, long hair could not be tolerated), stop dancing, wear whiteman's clothing, and to substitute the 4th of July, Christmas and Thanksgiving for native ceremonies. Farming was approved as an occupation.

The population of the Mescalero reservation includes members of other Apache tribes—Lipans, Mimbrenos and Chiricahuas—the latter arriving in 1913 after their release from prison in Ft. Sill, Oklahoma.

Today most Mescaleros earn their living by wage work on and near the reservation. Tribal income is derived from tourist facilities, hunting and fishing licenses, timber and cattle. Plans are being pushed to continue development of resources to provide more jobs for the Mescaleros.

Except for cradleboards and beadwork, Mescalero crafts have almost disappeared.

SUGGESTED READING

Sonnischsen, C. L. *The Mescalero Apaches.* U. of Oklahoma Press. Norman, 1958.

Stanley, F. *The Apaches of New Mexico, 1540-1940.* Pampa, Texas. 1962.

PHOTOGRAPHS BY WESTERN WAYS

Papago weavers produce more baskets than any other tribe in the United States.

PAPAGO *(pä'-pä-gō) — derived from "Papahvi-o-otam", the Pima name for this tribe which means "bean people". Native name is Toho'no-o-otam meaning "Desert People".* **Language** *- Piman.* **Reservations** *- Papago - 2,773,357 acres; San Xavier - 71,095 acres; Gila Bend - 10,297 acres.* **Population** *- (total) 12,000; resident - 6,000.* **Government** *- constitution adopted in 1937. Three reservations constitute eleven districts. Adult members of each district elect two persons to tribal council. Tribal council then elects tribal officers. Each district has a 5-man council.* **Celebrations:** *June 24 - San Juan's Day celebration - dances and chicken pulls in some villages. Oct. 4 - annual pilgrimage to festival in Magdalena, Sonora. Sahuaro wine festivals - during July (no specific dates). Annual rodeo and craft fair - late October.*

The Papago occupy today roughly the same area they inhabited at the time of Spanish contact. The members of this desert tribe are found in widely scattered villages in southern Arizona and northwestern Sonora.

Father Kino began his missionary work among the Papago in 1687. In addition to a new religion, the Indians acquired from the missions European crops, cattle, and horses and in a short time became proficient cattlemen.

Catholicism, in a modified form which centered about the worship of Saint Francis Xavier as a source of magical power, did not replace native beliefs but was merely added to them.

Each Papago village was politically autonomous, led by a headman called "The Keeper of the Smoke". A council of old men discussed village affairs but took no action until agreement was unanimous. Leaders for hunting and war gained their positions through personal ability and knowledge of rituals (obtained from dreams) necessary for success.

All villages had two locations; from spring until the fall harvest the Papago lived near the mouth of an arroyo where flash floods provided moisture for their fields. Cultivating flood plains provides, at best, a precarious livelihood so great use was made of desert plants, particularly the sahuaro fruit and mesquite bean. The winter villages

In late June Papago families move to their sahuaro camps to gather the fruit of the giant cactus.

Typical Papago village in southern Arizona.

TAD NICHOLS

Papago coiled baskets and figurines made of yucca, bear grass and devil's claw.

K. C DEN DOOVEN

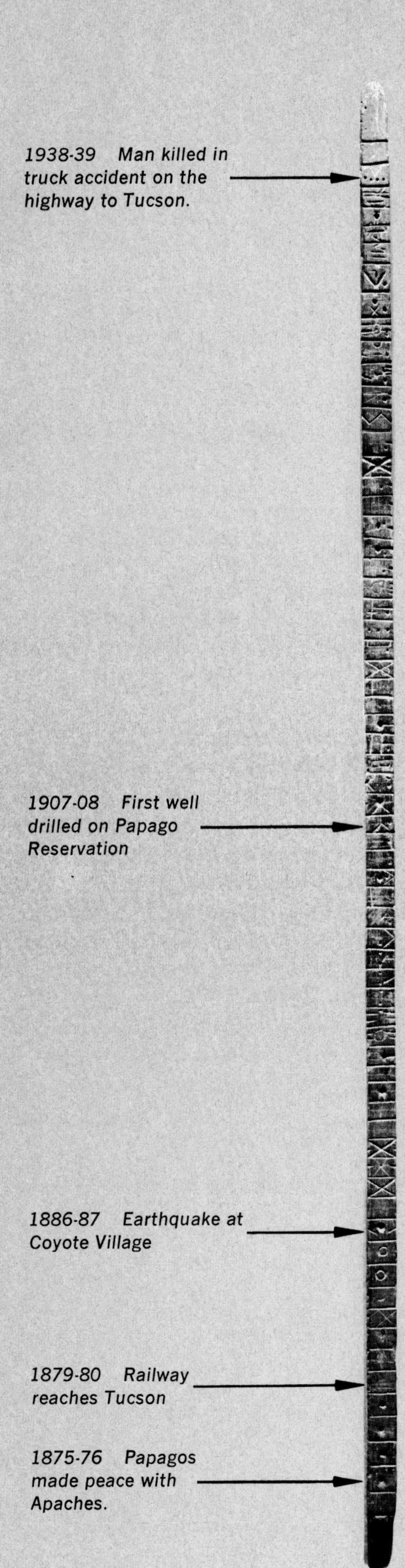

were located near mountain springs where the Papago hunted deer. In time of famine whole families moved north to the Pima villages where they earned their keep by helping the Pimas with their crops.

Papago territory came under American control with the Gadsden Purchase in 1853. The Indians lived peacefully under the new government despite occasional skirmishes with white cattlemen who appropriated Papago grazing land and water holes. For mutual protection against Apache raids they allied themselves with the Anglo settlers.

Because the Papagos had never fought against the U.S., they had no treaty which would protect them against encroachment by whites (there's a moral in this somewhere). In 1874 and 1882 two small reservations were finally set aside for the Papagos at San Xavier and Gila Bend. In 1917 the Sells reservation, the second largest in the U.S., was established. For many years it had the distinction of being the only Indian reservation in which the mineral resources did not belong to the tribe—a testimonial to the power of Arizona's mining industry.

Today less than one-third of the Papagos live on their reservation the year round. Many find work in nearby towns; others find seasonal jobs as agricultural workers. Cattle raising is the main source of income for those on the reservation.

Inadequate educational opportunities have greatly hampered these people in improving their economic situation. Tribal income from recent mining leases may help correct this.

The Papagos produce more basketry today than any other tribe. Coiled baskets in a variety of shapes, made of devil's claw and yucca sewn over a bundle of bear grass, are the most popular kind. Willow baskets and horsehair miniatures are also produced. Other crafts include horsehair lariats, carved wooden bowls and pottery.

SUGGESTED READING

Underhill, Ruth. *The Papago Indians of Arizona.* U.S. Indian Service. Haskell Institute. Lawrence, Kansas 1941.

Underhill, Ruth. *Papago Indian Religion.* Columbia University Press. New York, 1946.

Underhill, Ruth. *Autobiography of a Papago Woman.* American Anthropological Assn. Memoirs, No. 48, 1936.

Papago Calendar Stick from the village of Sil Nakya records the years from 1874 to 1940. The markings are not "writing" but merely mnemonic devices to remind the maker of specific events. Dots and circles usually represent major ceremonies. Seemingly mundane events such as the building of the first cement watering trough are also noted.

K. C. DEN DOOVEN

Yaqui pascola masks, rattle, rasping stick with sounding gourd, and drum; strings of cocoon rattles wrap around the dancers' legs.

YAQUI ***(yä'-kee) origin of name unknown.*** **Language** ***- Piman.*** **Population** ***- (Arizona only) - 3,000.*** **Reservation** ***- none. The Yaquis occupy six small villages; one each in Tucson, Tempe, Marana, Scottsdale and Eloy. Pascua village, formerly in Tucson, has now moved south of the city to occupy a tract of land given to it by the federal government.*** **Ceremonies** ***- Christmas, Saint's Days and Easter week (includes deer dancers, pascolas, matachines and chapeyekas).***

The Yaquis who occupy seven small villages in southern Arizona are political refugees from Sonora, Mexico.

This tribe of agriculturalists numbered about thirty thousand at the time of Spanish contact in 1533. Their rancherias were strung out along the full length of the Rio Yaqui. Formidable in battle and fiercely independent, they successfully resisted Spanish efforts to subdue them. Nevertheless they preferred to live in peace and signed a treaty with the Spaniards in 1610. At the request of the Yaquis, the Jesuits established missions in their settlements and the scattered population was eventually concentrated in eight towns. Under the Jesuit program agricultural practices were improved and new crops and livestock introduced. The Yaqui were surprisingly receptive to Catholicism and eagerly embraced the new religion. They also accepted the Spanish system of village government but considered themselves independent of Spanish authority. The Spaniards, reluctant to challenge this powerful tribe, were content to allow the Yaquis to remain autonomous and exempted them from taxation. Except for one revolt in 1740, caused by an influx of settlers and a conflict of interest between the Jesuits' program and civil authorities, the Yaquis remained at peace with the Spaniards.

After the War of Independence the Mexican government, wishing to integrate the Indians into the political and economic system, declared the Yaquis to be full citizens of the country. The change in status meant that they now had to pay taxes, something the Yaquis strongly objected to. This began a period of conflicts which continued for over a hundred years and ranged from extended guerrilla warfare to full scale battles. Attempted solutions to the Yaqui problem included peace offers, wholesale deportation of Yaquis to distant parts of Mexico, and military campaigns to exterminate resistance forces. The last skirmish occurred in 1927. It was during the last forty years of this period that many Yaquis sought asylum in Arizona.

Because of their political status, the Yaquis in Arizona are not treated as wards of the U.S. and are not entitled to any services from the Bureau of Indian Affairs. Many are now U.S. citizens but still maintain cultural ties with the villages in Sonora.

The Arizona Yaquis support themselves mainly as agricultural and construction workers. A language barrier and lack of educational opportunities have prevented significant economic advancement.

Yaqui religious life, a combination of native and Catholic beliefs and ceremonies, is still very strong. Public performances occur on Saints' days, Easter and Christmas.

SUGGESTED READING

Painter, Muriel T. *Faith, Flowers and Fiestas.* U. of Arizona Press. Tucson, 1962.

Spicer, Edward H. *Potam, A Yaqui Village in Sonora.* American Anthropological Assn. Memoir No. 77. 1954.

Spicer, Edward H. *Pascua, A Yaqui Village in Arizona.* U. of Chicago Press. Chicago, 1940.

Yaqui deer dancer and musicians.

TAD NICHOLS

PIMA *(pee'-mäh)* ***the name is derived from the native phrase "Pi-nyi-match" which means "I don't know". It was given as the answer to all questions asked by the first Spanish explorers who assumed the Indians were telling them their tribal name. The native name is "AH-KEE-MULT-O-O-TAM" meaning "River People".*** **Language -** ***Piman.*** **Reservations -** ***Gila River (shared with Maricopas) 371,932 acres; Salt River (shared with Maricopas) 46,619 acres; Ak Chin (shared with Papagos) 21,840 acres.*** **Population -** ***7,700.***

Pima willow and devil's claw baskets.

Hohokam, a Pima word meaning "those who have gone" is the name given to a remarkable agricultural people who occupied southern and central Arizona for about 1,500 years. Sometime after 1400 A.D. this culture, which had constructed elaborate irrigation systems in the Gila and Salt River valleys, declined and disappeared. Soon afterward it was replaced by Piman-speaking tribes, the Pima and Papago, who were possibly descended from the ancient Hohokam.

At the time of Spanish contact the Pima occupied the Gila River valley. These people were also agriculturalists who irrigated their farmlands with water diverted from the river. Their population, estimated at 2,500 in 1775, was concentrated in a number of permanent villages in the Gila valley. Although they had a strong sense of tribal unity, particularly in time of war, each village was politically independent.

The introduction of new crops and livestock were the only important Spanish contributions to Pima life. Lack of church funds prevented Kino's mission system from extending to their territory. The impact of a foreign religion was not felt until the late 1800's when the Pimas were converted to Presbyterianism.

Intensive contact with Anglos began during the Gold Rush when thousands of migrants to California passed through Pima territory. The Indians provided food and supplies for many of the travelers, and relations were consistently friendly.

After the Gadsden Purchase, Anglos began to settle in the rich farmlands of the Gila. Pima land rights were not recognized until 1859 when a reservation (much smaller than the territory they previously held) was established on the Gila. Serious problems began for the Pimas as the settlers upstream diverted the river water for their own use. Formal protests to Congress proved useless. A government proposal to relocate the Pimas in Oklahoma was rejected, and instead, many of the Indians moved into the Salt River valley. To solve the Pima's water problem, Coolidge Dam was built on the Gila River; the project was a technical success but the legal rights to the water had a curious way of winding up in the hands of non-Indians.

Fractionated land holdings (the result of the government's early allotment program) and lack of funds to drill wells prevent most Pimas from operating individual farms. Instead they lease their tiny holdings to white farmers. A tribal farming operation could become successful if individual allotments could be combined.

The Pima are famous for their basketry, but today only a few women continue to make the fine willow and devil's claw baskets. Pottery, a polished red ware decorated with black designs, has almost died out entirely.

SUGGESTED READING

Castetter, Edward F. and Willis H. Bell. *Pima and Papago Indian Agriculture.* Inter-Americana Studies No. 1. U. of New Mexico. Albuquerque, 1942.

Russell, Frank. "The Pima Indians". *Annual Report*, Bureau of American Ethnology. No. 26. Washington, D.C. 1905.

Webb, George. *A Pima Remembers.* U. of Arizona Press. Tucson, 1959.

Colorado River Tribes

The Yuma, Mohave, Cocopa, and Maricopa are the remaining tribes of eight closely related groups which occupied the Colorado River and lower Gila River valleys. (The "missing" four lost their tribal identities when they merged with the existing tribes). They shared a common language—Yuman—and a common culture.

These people were primarily agriculturalists; crops of corn, beans, and pumpkins were raised on the fertile flood plains of the river. Wild desert plants (especially mesquite beans), small game, and fish supplemented their diet. Compared to other tribes life was relatively easy and their culture was correspondingly simple.

These groups maintained a strong sense of tribal identity although they lacked formal political organization. They lived in small, widely separated settlements strung out along the river bottoms. Although some recognized hereditary chiefs, the real leaders gained status through performance, but even these men had no formal authority. Religious organization was equally lacking; public ceremonies consisted of individuals singing song cycles which had been "learned" during dreams. Great emphasis was placed on the acquisition of power through dreams. Success in gambling, curing, or war depended solely on this source. Jimson weed was occasionally used to induce dreams.

Although they showed no interest in amassing personal wealth, intertribal warfare was a common occurrence. The acquisition of new farm lands and scalps (a source of supernatural power) led to most fighting. Battles were conducted in a highly formalized manner; long lines of warriors faced each other and, after a warm-up period of shouted insults, engaged in hand-to-hand combat using a potato masher shaped club with a spiked handle as the favorite weapon. Occasionally champions were picked to settle the dispute.

The dead were disposed of by cremation accompanied by the burning of personal property—a custom which appalled the early white settlers and which the Bureau of Indian Affairs attempted to suppress in favor of the more "civilized" burial.

Contact with the Spaniards was very limited and these tribes remained, for the most part, outside the Spanish sphere of influence.

The Treaty of Guadalupe Hidalgo in 1848 and the Gadsden Purchase in 1853 gave the U.S. jurisdiction over these tribes. The tribes objected to the ensuing encroachment on their lands by whites, but their formal mode of warfare was useless against soldiers with rifles.

Although none of these tribes had treaties with the U.S., reservations were established for them beginning in the 1860's. However, loss of tribal lands to white squatters continued as late as 1940 when the Fort Mohave reservation was opened to settlement by whites.

COCOPA

(kō'-kō-päh) name is derived from Kwi-ka-pa, the Mohave name for this tribe - meaning unknown.* Language - *Yuman.* Reservation - *528 acres.* Population - *600 (one half live in Mexico).* Government - *tribal council consisting of five members. Constitution adopted in 1964.

The Cocopa, the southernmost of the Yuman tribes, occupied the delta region of the Colorado River. This tribe, which was divided into three bands, had a total population of 3,000 at the time of Spanish contact in 1540.

They were considered less warlike than the Yuma and Mohave but often fought with these tribes over territorial disputes. They maintained friendly relations with other neighboring groups with whom they traded for pinon nuts, acorns, hides, and tobacco. Occasionally captives taken in battle were traded to the Spanish for horses though children were usually adopted by childless couples.

The Cocopa farmed less than other Yuman tribes and relied more heavily on wild desert foods.

Dreams were of great importance in predicting the future and as a source of power. To dream of water insured success as a warrior; a mockingbird indicated a future as an orator; the appearance of an owl in a dream forbode death. No course of action was taken if a dream predicted anything other than success. Jimson weed was used to induce dreams that would insure success in gambling.

Today the Cocopa raise cotton and do some subsistence farming. The most important source of income is derived from agricultural employment.

SUGGESTED READING

Gifford, E. W. "The Cocopa". *Publications in American Archaeology and Ethnology*. U. of California. 1933.

MOHAVE

(mō-häh'-vee) also spelled Mojave. Corruption of the native name Aha-makave - meaning "beside the water".* Language - *Yuman.* Reservations - *Fort Mohave - 23,669 acres; Colorado River (shared with other tribes) 265,858 acres.* Population - *1,570.* Government - *(Fort Mohave) - tribal affairs are handled by a combination tribal council and business committee elected by tribal members.

The Mohave occupy roughly the same territory today as they did in early times. Their settlements were scattered along the bottom lands on both sides of the Colorado River stretching from Cottonwood Island south to the peaks called The Needles. At the time of Spanish contact (1776) they numbered about 3,000.

Strongly nationalistic and warlike, the Mohave fought with neighboring tribes and often traveled great distances to make war on other groups. Most of these military expeditions were conducted out of a sense of curiosity about new lands and people rather than to acquire territory or booty. They maintained friendly relations with the Yuma, Chemehuevi, Western Apache, and the Yavapai. They regarded the Pima, Papago, Maricopa, and Cocopas as traditional enemies.

In the 1840's a wagon trail to the California goldfields ran through Mohave territory. Friction with the immigrants culminated in a full-scale attack on a wagon train in 1858.

The following year Fort Mohave was built to maintain peace. Five Mohave headmen were held as hostages at Fort Yuma as insurance against any outbreak; (according to the Anglo version of the story they were later killed while trying to escape). To impress the Mohaves with the futility of further resistance a head chief was sent to Los Angeles and Washington D.C. to observe the strength of the Americans. Duly impressed, he used his influence to convince the Mohaves to remain at peace with the whites.

The Fort Mohave reservation (which includes parts of California, Nevada, and Arizona) and the Colorado River reservation were set aside in 1865. Many Mohaves turned to farming but others drifted to nearby white communities to find work.

Today many Mohaves work in Needles, California. With the development of tribal lands, stock raising and farming are becoming increasingly important economic pursuits.

Some Mohave women still produce elaborate beaded capes but craft work has no economic importance. At last report the remaining woman potter, Annie Fields, had stopped producing pottery and clay figurines.

Mohave effigy jar.

Mohave clay dolls.

PHOTOGRAPHS BY K. C. DEN DOOVEN

Maricopa pottery; the long-necked vases are adapted from an early scalp jar form.

MARICOPA ***(mäh-rēe-kō'-päh) name is the Spanish version of the Yuma (or Pima) name for this tribe. The native name is Pipa' meaning "men" or Pipatsje ("people").*** **Language -** ***Yuman.*** **Reservations -** ***Gila River - 371,932 acres - shared with the Pima; Salt River - 46,619 acres - shared with Pima; (there are no Maricopa living on the Maricopa (or Ak Chin) reservation.)*** **Population -** ***200.*** **Government -** ***the tribe has no separate tribal government but participates with the Pima in tribal council organizations on their respective reservations.***

The Maricopa tribe originally occupied an area on the lower Colorado River but was driven out in pre-Spanish times by incessant inter-tribal warfare and gradually drifted eastward along the Gila River. In 1774 an estimated 1,500 Maricopas inhabited the middle Gila east of the present town of Gila Bend to the mouth of the Salt River. Under pressure from their traditional enemies, the Mohave and Yuma, they migrated farther east into Pima country.

During the 1800's they were joined by the remnants of other Yuman tribes which had been driven out of their lower Colorado River territory. These tribes were the Halchidhoma, Kohvana, Halyikawamai and the Kaveltcadom (also called the Opa or Cocomaricopa). Former identities were lost and they were referred to collectively only as Maricopa. Together they allied themselves with the Pimas for protection against their common enemies. In 1857 the decisive defeat of a Yuma and Mohave raiding party by the Pima and Maricopa ended their troubles with those two tribes.

In spite of close contact with the Pima, the Maricopa maintained a way of life typical of Colorado River Yumans. The weaving of cotton blankets on a horizontal loom and the use of a calendar stick to record events were two of the few traits they picked up from their neighbors. They produced pottery in quantity but depended upon the Pimas for baskets.

Little remains of the old culture today. A very small amount of finely polished red pottery is still produced. Native dances, curing rites, tribal organization, and the great emphasis on dreams are all things of the past.

Today the Maricopa earn their living by subsistence farming, cotton raising, wage work, and leasing land for non-Indian agricultural developments. Most individual land allotments are too small to be farmed economically.

SUGGESTED READING

Ezell, Paul H. *The Maricopa, An Identification from Documentary Sources.* U. of Arizona Anthropological Papers No. 6. U. of Arizona Press. Tucson, 1963.

YUMA ***(you'-mäh) — derived from the Pima name lum for this tribe. Native name is Quechan - a reference to the trail they followed in leaving a sacred mountain from which all Yuman tribes are believed to have descended.*** **Language -** ***Yuman.*** **Reservation -** ***Fort Yuma, 54,000 acres - most of this reservation lies in California - only 480 acres are in Arizona.*** **Population -** ***2,150 of which an estimated 30 persons live in Arizona.***

The Yuma occupied the bottom lands of the Colorado River between the territories held by the Cocopa and Mohave.

Early Spanish contact was limited to a brief visit by Hernando de Alarcon who sailed up the Colorado River to Yuma country in 1540. Father

Kino paused in the Yuma villages during his trip to California in 1698 only long enough to distribute "canes of authority" to a few leaders.

In 1779 the Franciscans sent Padre Garces with a military escort to establish missions in Yuma territory. The Indians, who had proved to be friendly when treated as equals, resisted this attempt to subjugate them. They were unwilling to give up either their land or independence in return for the dubious benefits of a new religion. In 1781 the Yumans destroyed the mission (located near the present town of Yuma) and killed the priests and soldiers. Except for the introduction of new crops Spanish contact had no influence on Yuman culture.

The discovery of gold in California resulted in an invasion of Yuman lands by thousands of "Forty-niners" on their way to the goldfields. Despite raids on Yuman gardens by the migrants and the pilfering from wagon trains by the Indians the situation remained relatively peaceful. Some enterprising Yumas even constructed rafts and provided ferry service to transport the whitemen across the Colorado River.

Any attempt to settle on Yuman lands, however, met with opposition. The earliest difficulties arose when Anglos tried to establish a ferry service in competition with the Yumas. By 1850 the Americans were demanding "protection" from the Indians, and a military outpost was established at Camp Yuma. The small detachment kept hostilities to a minimum but failed to prevent the whites from taking Yuma land.

Hostilities soon broke out and the army proceeded to subdue the Yumas. This was done not by military engagements but through the destruction of Yuma fields and settlements.

A reservation was established in 1884 for the Indians; much of the land is arid and unsuited for agriculture so the Yumas rely heavily on wage work to supplement their limited farming.

A few women still produce beaded items ranging from elaborate capes to necklaces, small pins, and belts but this is the only surviving craft.

SUGGESTED READING

Castetter, Edward F. and Willis H. Bell. *Yuman Indian Agriculture.* U. of New Mexico Press. Albuquerque, 1951.

Forbes, Jack D. *Warriors of the Colorado.* U. of Oklahoma Press. Norman, 1965.

Forde, C. Darryl. *Ethnography of the Yuma Indians.* U. of California Publications in American Archaeology & Ethnology. Vol. 2, No. 4, 1931.

Spier, Leslie. *Yuman Tribes of the Gila River.* U. of Chicago Press. Chicago, 1933.

Yuma bow and arrows.

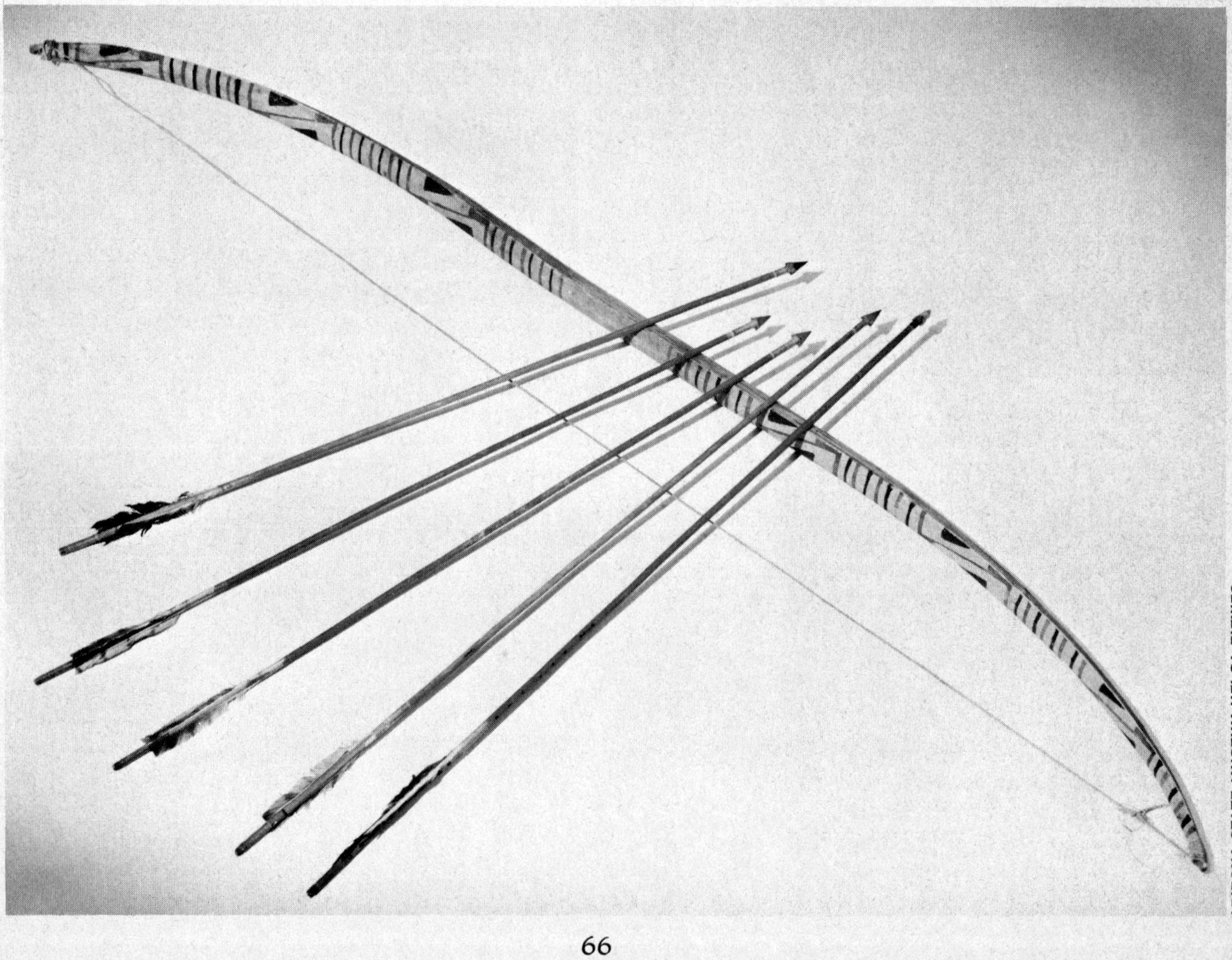

ARIZONA STATE MUSEUM-HELGA TIEWES

Hualapai baskets.

HUALAPAI ***(wäh'-läh-pie) also spelled Walapai - corruption of the native name Hah-wah-lah-pai-yah meaning "pine tree people". Language - Yuman. Reservations - Peach Springs and Big Sandy - 993,172 acres. Population - 675; resident - 425. Government - constitution adopted in 1938. Tribal council made up of eight elected members and one hereditary chief chosen by subchiefs of each band. Tribal officers are selected by the council.***

Originally the Pai occupied the area north of the Mohaves on the upper Colorado River. Long before the Spanish entered the Southwest they had moved eastward into the plateau region of northeastern Arizona. From this original group there emerged three separate tribes—Hualapai, Yavapai and Havasupai. Linguistically they are related to the Colorado River Yumans but culturally they more closely resemble the Southern Paiute.

The territory of the Hualapai included the area between Bill Williams River and the Grand Canyon and west almost to the Colorado River.

The Hualapai was a small tribe whose total population did not exceed one thousand. Their tiny settlements, usually consisting of two or three families, were scattered over the arid plateau wherever a permanent water supply was located. The Hualapai practiced a limited amount of agriculture but were mainly dependent upon game and wild plants for food.

Although they were not particularly warlike they occasionally fought with the Paiute and Yavapai. Friendly trade relations were maintained with the Mohave and the Hopi with whom they exchanged buckskins for foodstuffs and the Navajo from whom they obtained blankets.

Contact with the Spanish was limited to one brief visit by Father Garces in 1776 so that trouble with foreigners had to wait until the arrival of the Anglos in 1852.

At first relations with the Americans were peaceful but by 1866 feuds broke out when miners and cattlemen began to appropriate Hualapai springs and waterholes. To avoid bloodshed the Indians were moved to the Colorado River and placed on the Mohave reservation. Unaccustomed to the heat in the low country many sickened and died before the survivors moved back to their own land. However, during their two-year absence more of their territory had been taken by whites and the Hualapai were destitute, forced to accept government rations in order to exist. In 1883 a reservation was set aside for them in their native country, made up of those areas which the Anglos found unsuited to their own needs.

Because the Hualapai were not warlike and therefore not dangerous, the Anglos regarded them merely as an intolerable nuisance; one newspaper, the Mojave County Miner, in 1887 suggested editorially that rations for the Indians be mixed with "a plentiful supply of arsenic" to solve the problem.

Under the circumstances it is little wonder that the Hualapai eagerly took part in the Ghost Dance—a messianic movement started by Wovoka, a Paiute medicine man. For two years the prescribed dances were performed in the belief that they would result in the return of the Indian dead and the disappearance of the troublesome whites. Unfortunately (depending on your point of view) it failed.

Stock raising is the main livelihood for the Hualapai today. Except for limited acreage on the Big Sandy reservation most of the tribal land is unsuited for farming. Tribal income is derived mainly from timber sales. Because of limited natural resources most Hualapais must leave the reservation to earn a living.

Basketry, the only remaining native craft, continues to be produced. All Hualapai basketry employs a diagonal twining technique; bands of simple geometric patterns in aniline dye colors are the only decoration.

SUGGESTED READING

Dobyns, Henry F. and Robert C. Euler, *The Ghost Dance of 1889*. Prescott College Press. Prescott, 1967.

Kroeber, A. L. (ed.) "Walapai Ethnography" *Memoir* No. 42. American Anthropological Assn. 1935.

YAVAPAI *(yäh'-väh-pai)* — *the source of this name is in doubt - it may be derived from En-ya-va-pai-aa meaning "people of the sun" or Yawepe meaning "crooked mouth people" (i.e. "sulky").* **Language-** *Yuman.* **Population** *- 300.* **Reservations** *- Yavapai, 1,558 acres; Camp Verde - 577 acres (shared with Apache); Fort McDowell - 24,680 acres (shared with Apache).* **Government** *- Yavapai - informal community council. Camp Verde - constitution adopted in 1937. Tribal members elect 8-man community council which elects its own chairman and vice chairman. Fort McDowell - constitution adopted in 1936. Tribal members elect a five member community council.*

The Yavapai claimed as their territory the area from the Verde Valley to the Colorado River between the Gila and Bill Williams rivers. The tribe, which probably never numbered over 1,500, was divided into three subtribes, each made up of a number of smaller bands.

According to their tradition they once formed a single tribe with the Hualapai but intra-tribal hostilities brought about a split. Since that time the Hualapai were regarded as enemies along with the Havasupai, Maricopa, and Pima. They maintained friendly relations with the Western Apaches, particularly the Tonto band, with whom they frequently intermarried. As a result the Yavapai have often (and confusingly) been referred to as Mojave-Apache and Yuma-Apache.

Unlike their Yuman-speaking relatives on the Colorado River, the Yavapai practiced no agriculture but led a semi-nomadic existence subsisting entirely by hunting and gathering wild foods. Caves were used as dwellings in addition to brush shelters similar to the Apache wickiups.

Contact with the Spanish was very slight and the Yavapai managed to remain beyond the reach of both the Church and the Crown.

In the 1860's their territory was invaded by Anglo prospectors and miners. Bloody feuds and massacres resulted and continued until both the Yavapai and Apache were subdued by General Cook in 1872. In 1875 one thousand Yavapai were placed first at the Camp Verde army post and then moved to the San Carlos reservation. They remained at San Carlos for twenty-five years and then began to drift back to their home country. Some settled at Fort McDowell when they discovered their former lands had been taken over by white settlers. Others returned to Camp Verde where a small reservation was established for them in 1914. In 1935 a third reservation was set aside for Yavapais north of Prescott.

With the exception of the Fort McDowell reservation, which contains irrigated farm land, resources are extremely limited. Subsistence farming, stockraising and wage work make up their present economy.

Very fine coiled baskets, identical to those of the Western Apache in material, design, shape, and technique, are still occasionally produced.

SUGGESTED READING

Schroeder, Albert H. "A Brief History of the Yavapai of the Middle Verde Valley". *Plateau* Vol. 24, No. 3. Museum of Northern Arizona. Flagstaff, 1952.

Gifford, E. W. "Northeastern and Western Yavapai"., *Publications in American Archaeology and Ethnology* No. 34, U. of California. 1936.

Gifford, E. W. "The Southeastern Yavapai" Publications in American Archaeology and Ethnology. No. 29. U. of California 1932.

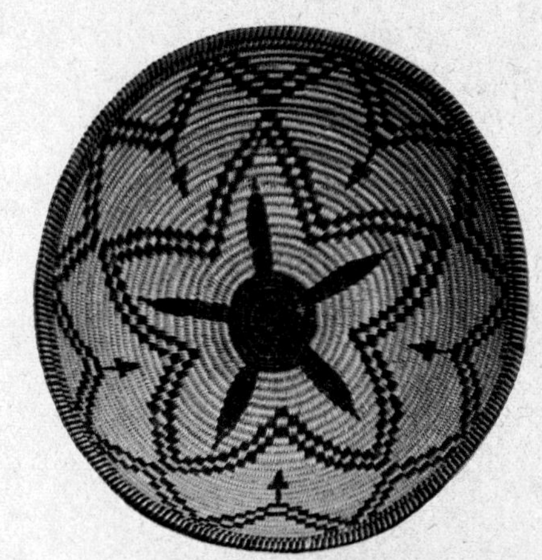

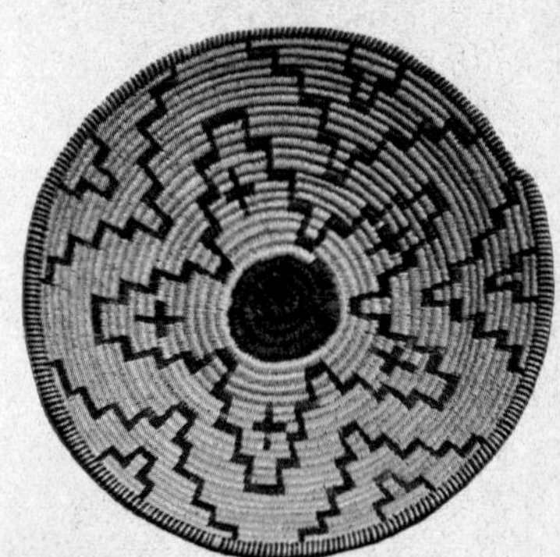

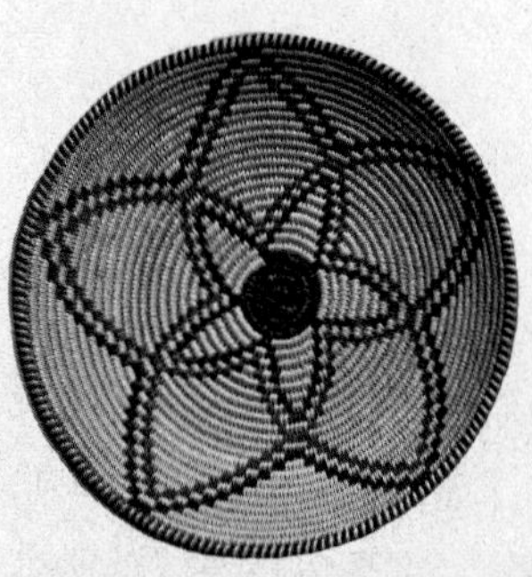

Yavapai baskets.

Aerial view of Havasu Canyon.

HAVASUPAI ***(häh-väh-soo'-pie) — derived from their tribal name Havasuwaipaa which means "Blue-green Water People". Also referred to as Supai and Coconino (Hopi name for these people). Language - Yuman. Reservation - 3,058 acres. Population - 250; resident - 168. Government - constitution adopted 1939. Tribal Council made up of four elected councilmen and three hereditary chiefs selected by subchiefs. Tribal officers selected by council. Ceremonies - Harvest Dance in late summer.***

The Havasupai, a branch of the Hualapai, separated from the main tribe during the 12th century A.D. to seek refuge from potential enemies and moved to the very bottom of the Grand Canyon. Today they are still the most isolated tribe in the U.S. Their reservation in Havasu Canyon can be reached only by foot or horseback over two long trails that lead down from the rim.

In early days the Havasupai occupied the canyon bottom only during the spring and summer months to farm their tiny gardens. In the fall, after the harvest, they moved to their winter dwellings on the plateau where they hunted deer, antelope, and mountain sheep. During the winter months the land along the riverbottom becomes cold and damp as the steep canyon walls shut out the sunshine.

Life among the Havasupai was simple. Rigid social and political organization was hardly necessary for a group with a population of less than 300. Religious activities were in the hands of medicine men who controlled the weather and disease and insured success in hunting and farming. A fall harvest dance was more a social reunion than a religious ceremony. Cremation of the dead and the destruction of the deceased's personal property (one of several customs which relates this tribe to the Yumans) was practiced until 1895 when the Bureau of Indian Affairs forbid this "uncivilized" practice.

Despite their isolation the Havasupai had considerable contact with the Hopi, trading buckskin, salt, and red mineral paint for agricultural products, textiles, and pottery. Padre Garces was the only Spaniard to visit (in 1776) this tribe. Plans to missionize the tribe failed to materialize. Contact with Anglos, which began in the 1850's was

Havasupai home. TAD NICHOLS

equally unimportant. No one, it seemed, coveted the isolated homeland of the Havasupai. In 1882 a reservation of 518 acres was established for the tribe in Havasu Canyon. The Havasupai refrained from requesting a larger tract in the belief that holding title to a greater area would invite trouble with the Anglos; a tiny reservation would be no temptation to even the most land hungry white-man.

Although often referred to as a "Shangri-la" by the casual visitor, the reservation is considerably less idyllic to those who live there. Agriculture, once the main occupation of the tribe, today only supplements the income derived from outside wage work. A few Havasupai earn a livelihood by providing transportation (horses and mules) and accommodations to infrequent visitors to their canyon.

Baskets, in both twined and coiled techniques, are still produced by the Havasupai but in very limited quantities.

SUGGESTED READING

Cushing, Frank H. *The Nation of Willows*, Northland Press. Flagstaff, 1965.

UTE ***(yōōt) derived from Yuta the Shoshoni and Comanche name for this tribe. Native name is Nunt'z meaning "the people". Language - Shoshonean. Reservations: Southern Ute Reservation (Colo.) 302,000 acres, Ute Mountain Reservation (Colorado and New Mexico) 555,000 acres. Uintah and Ouray Reservation (Utah) 852,411 acres. Population - (total) 3,500. Government - Southern Ute - constitutional form of government provides for election of a six member tribal council.***

The Utes today occupy reservations in three states: Utah, Colorado, and New Mexico. This distribution is indicative of the tremendous area that was once claimed by the ten (or more) bands which made up this tribe. Their territory stretched from the Great Salt Lake southwest to the Four Corners region and included most of Colorado and portions of northern New Mexico.

Originally these people lived in small family groups and subsisted, in the manner of most Great Basin tribes, by hunting and gathering. Linguistically they are related to the Chemehuevi and Paiute. Culturally they were closely related to the Southern Paiute until they acquired horses from the Spaniards in the early 1800's. Then they extended their hunting range onto the buffalo plains where they picked up traits typical of the Plains Indian cultures. This new mobility also allowed the family groups to unite into bands as the political and social units. A single Ute "tribe" as a political organization did not exist although bands might occasionally join forces to meet a common enemy.

The Ute maintained friendly relations with the Jicarilla Apache, Shoshoni, and Paiute; traded with the northern Rio Grande Pueblos; and warred with the Navajo, Kiowa, Cheyenne, Comanche, and Sioux. At one time they even joined with the Spanish in a temporary alliance against the Comanches.

Although contact with Europeans began in 1776 with a visit from Father Escalante, the Utes felt little effect from white contact until the mid-

ANTHROPOLOGY MUSEUM—U.N.M.

Ute basket weavers.

Southern Ute crafts.

1800's when American settlers began to move into their territory.

From 1849 through the 1880's, the Americans made—and broke—a series of treaties with the Utes. After Colorado became a state in 1876, a public clamor was raised to remove the Utes to provide more land for whites. Each demand resulted in a new treaty and less land for the Utes until one chief was led to ask sarcastically if the U.S. lacked the power to enforce its own treaties. (General Grant once described a reservation as "a piece of land set aside for Indians and entirely surrounded by white thieves".) That the displacement of the Utes took place with a minimum of bloodshed is a tribute to Ouray, a leader of the Southern Utes, who recognized the futility of warring against overwhelming odds.

With the loss of their best hunting grounds the Utes became dependent upon government rations during their early reservation years.

Today the Southern Utes, made up of the Wiminuche, Capote, and Moache bands, occupy two reservations in southwestern Colorado and a small part of New Mexico. Farming, stock raising, and sheepherding provide their main livelihood. Tribal income, derived from gas and oil leases and money obtained from a land claims settlement with the U.S. government, is being used to develop rangelands and purchase off-reservation ranches to improve the economic standard of the people.

Little remains of the native culture; the Bear Dance, an annual spring ceremony, and the Sun Dance (derived from Plains tribes) are now largely social gatherings. A number of the Ute Mountain group are members of the Native American Church.

Crafts are becoming increasingly scarce, but beaded buckskin bags, belts, and moccasins are still being made along with some coiled basketry.

SUGGESTED READING

Aberle, David F. and Omer C. Stewart "Navaho and Ute Peyotism". *Series in Anthropology* No. 6. U. of Colorado Press, 1957.

Emmitt, Robert. *The Last War Trail.* U. of Oklahoma Press. Norman, 1954.

Opler, Morris K. "The Southern Utes" in Ralph Linton (ed) *Acculturation in Seven American Indian Tribes.* New York, 1940.